The Spiritual Journey

The Spiritual Journey

*Critical Thresholds and Stages
of
Adult Spiritual Genesis*

by

*Marie Theresa Coombs, Hermit
and
Francis Kelly Nemeck, O.M.I.*

A Michael Glazier Book
THE LITURGICAL PRESS
Collegeville, Minnesota

A Michael Glazier Book published by The Liturgical Press

Cover design by David Manahan, O.S.B. Detail of icon of the Holy Trinity by Andrei Rublëv, ca. 1410, Historical Museum, Moscow.

<u>   12</u>

Library of Congress Cataloging-in-Publication Data

Coombs, Marie Theresa.
    The spiritual journey : critical thresholds and stages of adult spiritual genesis / by Marie Theresa Coombs and Francis Kelly Nemeck.
        p.   cm.
    "A Michael Glazier book."
    Originally published: Wilmington, Del. : M. Glazier, 1987.
    Includes bibliographical references.
    ISBN 0-8146-5546-7
    1. Spiritual life—Catholic authors. 2. Conversion. I. Nemeck, Francis Kelly, 1936- . II. Title.
    BX2350.2.C623   1993
    248.4′82—dc20   93-9680
                                                                                  CIP

To

Christ Jesus:
the Way, the Truth and the Life

in

Loving Memory
of
May Yeary Nemeck
(1907-1984)

Whose life and death taught us
so much about the mystery which
we treat herein:

namely,

"That, although outwardly we are
fading away, inwardly we are being
transformed day by day" (2 Co 4:16).

Table of Contents

Final Thresholds

Principal Abbreviations and General Notes

Ascent St. John of the Cross. *The Ascent of Mount Carmel.* Various editions, publications and translations.

Canticle St. John of the Cross. *The Spiritual Canticle* (2nd redaction). Various editions, publications and translations.

Contemplation Nemeck, Francis Kelly and Coombs, Marie Theresa. *Contemplation* (Michael Glazier, Inc., 1935 West Fourth Street, Wilmington, DE 19805), 1982.

C. Prayer Merton, Thomas. *Contemplative Prayer.* New York: Image Books D285, 1971.

D. Milieu Teilhard de Chardin, Pierre, *The Divine Milieu.* New York: Harper Torchbooks 384, 1965.

Flame St. John of the Cross, *The Living Flame of Love* (2nd redaction). Various editions, publications and translations.

Night St. John of the Cross. *The Dark Night of the Soul.* Various editions, publications and translations.

PL Migne, J.P., ed. *Patrologia Latina.* Turnhout: Brepols.

Receptivity Nemeck, Francis Kelly. *Receptivity* (Vantage Press, Inc. 516 West 34th Street, New York, N.Y. 10001), 1985.

Spiritual Direction   Nemeck, Francis Kelly and Coombs, Marie Theresa. *The Way of Spiritual Direction* (Michael Glazier, Inc., 1935 West Fourth Street, Wilmington, DE 19805), 1985.

Writings Teilhard de Chardin, Pierre, *Writings in Time of War*. New York: Harper and Row, 1968.

Note 1: All translations from Hebrew, Greek, Latin, French and Spanish sources are our own. We frequently adapt these texts to reflect contemporary inclusive language.

Note 2: While we consistently use the term "Father" in this study in reference to God, we acknowledge the legitimacy of speaking of God as "Mother."

Note 3: Following the Western mystical tradition we employ the word "soul" in this study as synonymous with "person," stressing the deepest recesses of that person. This usage does not come from the scholastic *corpus-anima* (body-soul) distinction, but rather is derived from the Hebrew *nephesh* (breath, person, soul) and the New Testament *psyche* (life, self, soul).

INTRODUCTION

The Spiritual Journey is a study of the thresholds and stages of adult interior development. It represents a descriptive or inductive approach to the mystery of God becoming all within the human person, rather than a prescriptive or deductive approach. This book is a sequel and a complement to our two previous works: *Contemplation* (1982) and *The Way of Spiritual Direction* (1985).

In *Contemplation*, we dealt specifically with the transition from discursive prayer to contemplative prayer. For most people, this is an especially difficult threshold to discern. In our present study we take up the gamut of interior genesis, particularly from the onset of what might be called "holistic adulthood" to personal death. We describe the successive stages of a person's interior evolution as evidenced in the spiritual masters and in fellow pilgrims. Within these stages, we further concentrate on the prayer dimension of each passage together with the principles necessary to discern its authenticity. Thus, our new study will help situate our previous work on contemplation in the broader context of overall adult interior development.

In *The Way of Spiritual Direction*, we presented a theological and pastoral exposition of that all important ministry within the Christian community, stressing the contemplative dimension required to effectively exercise that gift. In this present work, basing ourselves on considerable experience and research, we afford directors the principles of discernment which they need in order to guide their directees through the various stages of spiritual genesis.

Most of these principles have been known for hundreds of years, especially since the publication of the writings of St. Teresa of Jesus (1515-1582) and St. John of the Cross (1542-1591). But these principles need to be synthesized anew and freshly presented for the man and woman of the twenty-first century, particularly in the light of developmental psychology and the social sciences.

A few attempts along these lines have been made recently. Some have proven more thorough than others. Yet, practically all these attempts treat only the beginning stages of adult spiritual development. Those which do venture further remain sketchy when it comes to the more advanced stages of prayer.

We specifically limit our study to *adult* spiritual genesis. A great deal of interior development obviously takes place throughout infancy, childhood and adolescence. This development constitutes the foundation of adult spiritual progress. Nonetheless, we leave the treatment of the critical thresholds and stages pertaining to the earlier phases of human life to authors more experienced than ourselves in these areas. Although we do discuss the critical threshold of individual creation — the direct bringing into being by God of a human person — we then presuppose all the stages between that instant and the onset of a certain holistic adulthood. We use the term "holistic adulthood" to describe that phase of life wherein an individual is well on the way to becoming his/her own person in all basic respects: emotional, psychological, moral, spiritual, etc. Adulthood in this sense does not happen in a flash or automatically at the age of eighteen or twenty-one. It can occur earlier for some people and much later for others. A person who is legally an adult is not necessarily also a holistically mature adult. These distinctions are evident to any discriminating reader.

Using the basic terminology and insights of John of the

Cross and Pierre Teilhard de Chardin (1881-1955), we rein-terpret and re-present in the light of contemporary research the critical thresholds and stages of adult spiritual genesis. These begin with the inception of reflective discursive prayer and pass on through spiritual marriage. Needless to say, not every adult is drawn by God through all these thresholds this side of death. But, as any experienced spirit-ual director can attest, God does lure countless ordinary men and women into the later stages of mystical prayer —sometimes without their even adverting to the fact.

Be that as it may, as we grow older we become increas-ingly aware of the truth that, although the exterior dimen-sions of our lives are slipping away, the deep spiritual core of our being is flourishing as never before (2 Co 4:16). If all could only perceive this mystery and rejoice in it!

"Lord, that I may see" (Lk 18:41).

FOUNDATIONS

Chapter 1

SPIRITUAL GENESIS

There are many aspects to the human person: familial and private; social and individual; ecclesial and civil; physical, emotional, psychological and spiritual. All these aspects interact and complement one another. They all contribute to an integrated life. Yet, the older a person grows, the more these diverse dimensions converge upon and are ultimately synthesized in one: the spiritual.[1]

From the moment of inception[2] to death, each person evolves towards increasing spiritualization. Spiritualization is the process of our transformation in God, by God, so as to bring us to consummate union in love with him.[3] Dwelling within our innermost being, Father, Son and Spirit deify us. The indwelling Trinity divinizes, sanctifies and regenerates us, gradually re-creating us as beloved children of the Father (Rm 8:15-16), in the image of Christ Jesus (2 Co 3:18), according to the Spirit of God (Rm 8:2-6).[4]

The process of spiritualization is, therefore, rightly called a "genesis." Derived from the New Testament *ginomai*, genesis means becoming, developing, evolving, but not just

---

[1]See *Spiritual Direction*, pp. 25-31.

[2]We frequently use the term "inception" rather than "conception" to refer to the instant when God creates the human person within the matter prepared by the cocreative activity of one's parents. This moment coincides presumably with conception. Nonetheless, we wish to respect legitimately differing viewpoints. "Inception," therefore means whenever the human person as such actually begins.

[3]See *Contemplation*, pp. 16-18.

[4]See *Spiritual Direction*, pp. 15-24.

any which way. Genesis denotes an inner movement towards the highest possible degree of being, towards ultimate consummation in God.[5]

All creation is in spiritual genesis (Rm 8:22). Each individual creature according to its own mode of being, as well as creation as a whole, is brought into existence by the Word (Jn 1:3; Col 1:16) so as to be recapitulated in Christ (Col 1:20). All creation is in a spiritual direction which has but one term: God himself.[6] And "God is Spirit" (Jn 4:24).

Each person has a unique spiritual direction. We are called to transforming union in God in such a way that each individual personality reaches in God the fullness of stature, the consummate blossoming of uniqueness and freedom. This is spiritual genesis at its term. However, this side of death spiritual genesis is a slow, all-embracing process. Every person, event and circumstance of our daily life contribute somehow to that process. We are transformed inch by inch, drop by drop.

What happens then when these inches turn into miles and our cup begins to fill? What is the human experience at different points along the way to consummate union with God? It is precisely these questions which we address in this study of the thresholds and stages of adult spiritual genesis.

A threshold is far more than a milestone, however. A threshold occurs when the interior forces of convergence become so strong and concentrated that they produce a breakthrough, a new and improved mode of being. The birth of the United States in 1776 out of the original thirteen colonies is an example of such a process.

A threshold frequently possesses the characteristics of a crossroads, of a fork in the road. It calls forth a fundamental option and commitment of oneself to a particular direction. Lincoln's Emancipation Proclamation was such an advance for the struggling Union.

A threshold does not necessarily take place in one fell

---

[5]See P. Teilhard de Chardin, *"Letter to Fleming"* (May 19, 1954); *Receptivity*, pp. 10-11 (n. 11).

[6]See *Spiritual Direction*, pp. 27-31.

swoop. This is evident in the struggle for civil rights during the sixties. And, although a threshold marks the emergence of a new mode of being, certain aspects of the previous mode may persist and, therefore, still be in need of further renewal. The continued struggle for civil rights throughout the seventies and into the eighties exemplifies this fact.

A threshold is distinguishable from the stage which precedes it and the one which follows it as a doorway separates two adjacent rooms. Sometimes a threshold blends imperceptibly with the two stages which it divides. At other times, while resembling the stage that it introduces, the threshold stands in marked contrast to the one which precedes it. While a threshold culminates all that goes before, its principal function is to catapult a particular movement into a new mode of being. Thus, all the dynamics of a threshold press forward rather than backward. Thus also, some thresholds are scarcely distinguishable from the stages which they introduce: adolescence, for example.

A given stage may comprise several phases. Each phase indicates a further development within the same stage. There may be, for instance, initial phases, settling-in phases and advanced phases.

A. *Influences upon Spiritual Progress*

Of all that we do and undergo throughout life, which things specifically influence our interior development? What has bearing on our transformation in God? The response is emphatic: Everything! Literally every person, every occurrence, every joy, every pain, every hope, every disappointment, every success and every failure enter somehow into our spiritual progress. "We know that God converts everything into good for those who love him" (Rm 8:28). Nothing actual or imaginable escapes his divine providence (Rm 8:38-39).

God integrates everything that happens to us throughout life into our personal salvation history. Not everything, of course, is immediately good, but there is nothing conceivable that is not capable of becoming good for those who love God and believe in him.[7] Not even sin! Whether it is a question of our own personal sin or the sinfulness of others affecting us (for example: their hatred, revenge, envy), good can emerge from it. God's will for us is accomplished with equal facility on his part whether we say yes or no to him. God will not allow his word to return to him empty, without carrying out what it was sent to do (Is 55:10-11). However, the sooner and more wholeheartedly we abandon ourselves to God's loving initiative, the more we avoid the unnecessary grief and tension which our resistance heaps upon us.

The above truth needs some explaining. How God moves us to will ever more freely what he himself wills for us is one of the great mysteries of Christianity (Rm 11:33-34). In fact, Ephesians and Colossians refer to it as "*the* mystery" (Eph 1:9; Col 1:26). We can never adequately express how our freedom of choice accords with God's freedom of election (Rm 8:28-30). Certain theologies of this mystery tend towards either of two extremes.

The first extreme is predicated upon a static world view: From all eternity, God has drawn up a blueprint of our lives which we follow inexorably from conception to death. It is as if he programs us, as if the pursuit of our vocation were little more than the execution of an internal tape or of a divinely-inserted floppy disk. God and his will are considered immutable. Everything we do and become fits a priori into his plan.

The second extreme view is that of the fatalist. It postulates that all creation fends for itself; that God throws us into one gigantic cosmic arena and lets us fight it out. Only the fittest survive. God rewards the morally strong with heaven, while he leaves the failures to fall away.

In reality, the manner in which God's providence cooperates with us in everything — always producing not only what is good for us, but ultimately what is best — is other than the two tendencies mentioned above. Six principles

[7]See *Receptivity*, pp. 89-103, 120-121.

shed particular light on reevaluating the cooperation of divine providence in our evolving lives.

(1) A first principle to remember in discussing this mystery is that our mode of speaking about it is sorely limited. For example, to say that God changes or that he is changeless is to speak in anthropomorphisms. In reality, God neither changes nor is he changeless in the way these terms apply to our human experience. The dynamics of change and the stability of changelessness coexist preeminently in God. Moreover, what we experience in life as dynamic and as stable are created participations in divine attributes.

God is God. Nothing that we can ever say of him is capable of expressing him as he is in himself. The best that we can do is to speak of him analogically, always aware that there remains greater dissimilarity than similarity in whatever we say of him. Furthermore, God's communication with us through concepts and language is also by way of analogy. While some analogies are more meaningful than others — "I am the way, the truth and the life"(Jn 14:6); "God is Spirit" (Jn 4:24); "God is love" (1 Jn 4:16) — he infinitely transcends whatever we predicate of him. God is always other than what we say he is.

(2) A second principle in addressing this mystery is the fact that God really does "co-operate" with us — *syn-ergei* (Rm 8:28) — in everything, converting it into our good. He works together with us in every detail of our lives: in each choice, in everything we do, in everything that happens to us.

(3) A third principle necessary to arrive at some understanding of divine providence is this: What we call "the here and now" — space, time, movement — is a mortal participation in eternity. What we experience as past, present and future is a this-life participation in now-eternal: the dynamic *nunc stans et semper manens.*

(4) A fourth principle that requires serious pondering is the one expressed in the conclusion of deutero-Isaiah. Yahweh speaks: "The word which proceeds from my mouth does not return to me empty. It does not come back to me without carrying out my will and actually succeeding in

what it was sent to accomplish" (Is 55:11). St. Paul reiterates even more specifically this same truth in his hymn to divine love: "With God on our side who can be against us?" No created being "can ever separate us from the love of God" made incarnate "in Christ Jesus Our Lord" (Rm 8:31,35,39).

(5) A fifth principle which sheds some understanding on the workings of divine providence is couched in the parable which Jeremiah acted out in symbolic gesture shortly before the destruction of Jerusalem: his visit to the potter. Whenever the vessel that the craftsman was working on turned out other than he had intended, he would start from there and mold it into another vessel. In this action, Jeremiah perceived Yahweh's word: "Can I not accomplish with you what this potter does? Yes, as the clay is in the potter's hand, so you are in mine" (Jer 18:4-6). When we turn out "wrong," God continues to work with us, molding us, forming us in his image.

(6) Finally, a sixth principle concerns vocation. There is a universal call to holiness. Each person is called by God to transforming union in love. But what is usually termed "vocation" refers to an individual's particular call within that general call: one's unique way to transforming union.

We receive our fundamental vocation in life simultaneously with God's initial act of creating us. Our vocation is integral to who, how and what we are to become. Our vocation is so much a part of our personhood that we can never really become whoever we are meant to be unless we become in a certain way. We experience our vocation as an existential inability to do/be/become otherwise. It is something inescapably "burning in my heart, imprisoned in my bones. I cannot indefinitely muster the effort to restrain it" or deny it, or thwart it (Jer 20:9).

The prophets refer to God's irresistible call to us in statements like the following: "I have called you by your very own name. You are mine" (Is 43:1). Jesus himself proclaims: "You did not choose me. No, I have chosen you" (Jn 15:16).

All the preceding principles emanate from and converge upon this mysterious and complex truth: God works with us every step of our journey towards transforming union in him. God has also implanted in all nature a multitude of laws which govern the diverse aspects of the evolutionary process. He lets nature take its course, but in so doing God integrates everything that happens into our collective as well as individual salvation history. Thus, God is immanent every inch of the whole way, in every instant of time.

God's cooperation with us is also operative in what people refer to as "chance." Much of what is commonly called "chance" is in reality part of nature and is governed by nature's laws, even if these laws remain obscure (for example, why lightning strikes a specific place). Chance is the incalculable element in human existence. It is that which happens unpredictably without discernible intention or observable cause. St. John of the Cross esteems his prison break in 1578 a "happy chance."[8] This phrase furthermore refers to the breakthrough which God himself effected in John's soul. Hence it is also "a blessed grace." All chance falls within God's providence. Nothing imaginable can happen to us that he does not convert into good.[9] But only deep faith enables us to appreciate this truth.

When we cooperate with God's grace and the laws of nature, he obviously works with us. When we resist his grace and act contrary to nature's laws, he still works with us but in a way different than had we not sinned. God adapts his providence second by second to all the converging circumstances of our lives at any point along the way.

Three examples may help put some flesh and blood on these principles. A word of caution, however. Examples such as these can also obscure the truth that they are meant to convey: *Exempla claudicant.* The reader could conceivably imagine innumerable possibilities and extenuating circumstances for each of these stories. We intend them to be understood like simple parables expressing only a basic lesson or moral.

(1) Given the laws of statistical probability, sooner or

---

[8] *O dichosa ventura*, poem *In a Dark Night*, stanzas 1 and 2. See *Receptivity*, pp. 32-36.

[9] See *Receptivity*, pp. 89-103. (esp. 96-97).

later an airliner is going to crash. If I happen to be on that flight, I will go down with the plane. God does not specifically arrange that I take that particular flight. Nor does he cause the plane to crash. But given the fact that I am at the point of imminent death, God works within me accordingly.

Suppose, however, that the pilot manages to crash-land the plane, and that I am located in the tail section which breaks off upon impact. The section that I am seated in does not explode with the rest of the plane. Faced with these new circumstances, God works together with me in an entirely different way than he would have had I been engulfed in flames. Ordinarily, we would not say that God directly spared me, anymore than we would assert that he directly killed those who died in the explosion. No, I was spared because of where I was fortunate enough to be sitting: "O happy chance!" They died because of the fire where they were located. God works immanently and intimately with each one, exactly where each one is physically, morally, spiritually. Moreover, God works with and through all nature's laws: gravity, aerodynamics, geography, physics, engineering, etc.

(2) Another example: Suppose a young man grows up in a good Christian environment. His parents and friends urge him to study for the priesthood. Because he wants to serve God, help others and please his parents, the idea of the priesthood appeals to him. His seminary days pass routinely, without the young man confronting his real desires and motivations. He appears successful in his ministry, but has nagging doubts regarding his "chosen life." After much soul-searching and counsel this man comes to see that herein lies his problem: While he "chose" the priesthood because it seemed like the appropriate course to take, he never wholeheartedly committed himself to it. Moreover, he went along with clerical celibacy, without ever truly being able to integrate its exigencies into his personal life.

Let us suppose, furthermore, that God has actually given this young man a vocation to marriage, and may or may not have called him to presbyteral ministry. The young man makes his choices with relatively good faith all along the way. God cooperates with him in each of these options, although in the light of later maturity some of his decisions are perceived to have been mistaken, misguided or wrongly discerned. Eventually, this man realizes his vocation to marriage. He leaves the active ministry, takes a wife and proceeds to live as Christian a conjugal life as he can. God continues to work with him every step of the way both for his personal salvation as well as for that of his newfound family.

(3) A third example: God gives a young woman a contemplative vocation. He cooperates with her through First Communion, Confirmation and graduation with honors. Then, in college she turns up pregnant and on drugs. She keeps the baby, marries the father and substitutes alcohol for drugs. Life goes on: some joyful moments and some very painful moments. Eventually, she divorces her husband and marries another. This pattern recurs several times with her having a child or two in each marriage. God continues to work with her every step, every choice, every tear, every smile, developing the contemplative thrust within her. She may end up living the contemplative life only the last ten days before her death, as she lies in a charity ward dying of cirrhosis of the liver. But God was cooperating with her every instant from inception to the grave, converting everything to her good.

In any situation the what-if's and the what-might-have-been's are interminable. God never indulges in that game. He always co-operates (*syn-ergei*, Rm 8:28) with what is and with all that is here and now.

Yet, God not only works with events as they happen in our lives, he can also bring about events to bear directly on our spiritual development. God's purpose — his *prothesis* (Rm 8:28; 9:11; Eph 1:11; 3:11) — can initiate situations or modify them. He can directly bring together two persons whom he calls to marriage. He uses the natural process of sexual intercourse to bring into being the person he has foreordained from all eternity. Sometimes the parents are surprised, but there are no "accidents" where God's will is concerned.

Furthermore, God uses us as instruments of his providence in the lives of others. The unique vocation which each person possesses exists not only for his/her own sanctification, but also as a gift for many. There is a ministerial dimension to every vocation. God has a mission for everyone, even the stillborn child. God uses the process of our individual spiritualization — no matter how obscure — to assist others in their transformation. In a sense, we are all *charismata*.

There is still another dimension to divine providence. God does not limit himself exclusively to the concurrence of external and natural causes, even to directly accomplish his purpose. He cooperates with these and uses them as a catalyst for our spiritual development, but he can also work beyond them at any time for his own reasons.

For instance, if I am interiorly ripe for conversion, God will elicit that conversion regardless of exterior stimuli or circumstances. Another example: If I am interiorly ready to die — that is, if God has brought me to the exact point of qualitative preparedness that he wills for me — my heart will stop beating and remain arrested no matter how much CPR is applied. Conversely, if God is not ready for me to die — if I am not yet at the precise intensity of spiritualization that he desires for my passage into eternity — I will not be killed even if I step on a land mine or fall off a cliff. I may lose a leg or break my neck, but I will not die until God is ready for me to do so. We all know specific instances of this kind of divine activity. The popular, though inaccurate, term for it is "miraculous."

God never forces us to be or to do anything, although the power of his presence can be experienced as overwhelming and irresistible (Jer 20:7-9). Nature and humans can exert considerable violence at times, and God works with that too. But God himself is never violent. He inexorably moves us from within to become ultimately what he wills of us. He accomplishes this without any blueprints, tapes or floppy disks. He does it freely: freely on his part and freely on ours. True freedom is always towards the greatest good. And God is goodness itself.

God not only leaves us free, but also he immeasurably enhances our freedom to choose always what is best. When we abuse this freedom and choose to sin, he works with us towards repentance. God accomplishes this conversion so transcendently that we end up qualitatively where he wanted us all along in spite of our sin, and even in a sense because of our sin: *O felix culpa!*

How does God move us to will freely what he wills for us? How does God get exactly what he wants of us in the end: with us, through us, in spite of us and sometimes all three at the same time? How does God cooperate intimately with all the laws of nature, including chance, yet remain infinitely beyond them all? How does God harmonize at every instance of our earthly sojourn the intricate balance between our exterior-falling-into-decay and our interior-being-renewed-day-by-day? The response is: He does! And therein lies the mystery of his divine providence.

In these few considerations, we have in no way presented a comprehensive treatise of divine providence. We have merely tried to posit an attitude, an evolutionary view of God's cooperation with us in all things (Rm 8:28). Even questions related to his "foreknowledge" and his "predestination" (Rm 8:29) can be more faithfully understood in the light of this perspective.

"Foreknowledge" is our conceptualization and an anthropomorphism. This is so because we presently live and think in time. While God cooperates with our becoming in this life, he exists in eternity, the forever now. We know in terms of past, present and future. For God all knowledge is simply now. Time is a quantitative and progressive participation in the purely qualitative and dynamic simplicity of eternity. Yes, God knows us "before" he forms us "in the womb" (Jer 1:5). But that means: Knowing us, he causes us to begin becoming ourselves in him, in time, for eternity.

"Predestination" is also our conceptualization and an anthropomorphism. This is so because we move and operate in space. God does not decide in some static way beforehand who, how and what we shall be and then set us like robots on the course. He rather destines us in a dynamic manner to become freely deified even "before" we "come to birth" (Jer 1:5). His universal call to holiness is never definitively thwarted, because the Lord's word does not return to him empty (Is 55:10-11). All who are foreknown are therefore predestined. All who are predestined are also called. All who are called are futhermore transformed. And all who are transformed are ultimately divinized (Rm 8:30).

At best, what we see of God's providence is like looking at the underneath portion of a tapestry. There appear far more loose ends than patterns. Yet, God views the same tapestry of our lives right side up, not only from on high but also close up: every thread, every knot, every weave. After all, he cooperates with us in every detail.

This view of God's tender care for us is integral to our understanding of the thresholds and stages of adult spiritual genesis. Furthermore, this view sheds particular light on our cooperation with him (1 Co 3:9). For although we are the ones undergoing the successive thresholds, God himself brings about our spiritual genesis.

Thus, because God is with us, everything in our individual lives influences our spiritual progress: our sin as well as our virtue, our limitations as well as our gifts, our pains as well as our joys, our likes as well as our dislikes, together with all that we receive through heredity and environment. Nothing is too small, too fleeting, too banal, too insignificant to escape God's loving cooperation.

God writes straight with our crooked lines. His ways zigzag through all our categories, laws and conventions (Is 55:7-9). God is never limited, pinned down or frustrated by anything that we do or say or try to be. On the contrary, God integrates it all into our emerging transformation in him.

B. The Two Arms of God's All-embracing Love

God cooperates with us in all that we are, and do, and become. His providence is with us and within us from beginning to end as well as every inch and every instant along the way.

Transforming union, on the one hand, and the dark night of our soul, on the other, comprise the totality of God's influence upon us and from within us.[10] Both interact with each other beginning with inception and reaching their respective climaxes in death. If we were to try to imagine these two interacting influences, we would describe them as the two arms of God's all-embracing love.

The dominant arm, of course, is that of transformation. Because God is so intent on transforming us in himself, he has to purge everything in us that cannot be transformed. Thus, our night is a direct result of his light. All that we suffer in life is not primarily either an expiation or a castigation. It is fundamentally the reverse side of loving communion. Moreover, if God does not purify us all at once, in one fell swoop, it is not because he cannot do so, but rather because we cannot take it. Our purification requires an entire lifetime.[11]

God's transforming and purifying embrace begins when I begin. At the moment of my individual creation I become a child of God destined to eternal love. In that instant also, God starts drawing good from all my natural and mortal limitations. My interior life is coextensive with my human life.[12]

I am a child of God from the instant that I become a child of my parents, a child of my time and a child of my world. The sacramental celebration of this mystery is Baptism.

From inception onward, God tightens his embrace. Not only does he make us more spiritual with each passing day, but also he purges us more intensely with each successive year. Finally, these two arms of his all-embracing love meet in our personal death.

Death occurs at the juncture where our outer, physical being has fallen completely into decay and our inner, trans-

[10]See *Contemplation*, pp. 16-18; *Receptivity*, pp. 36-41.
[11]See *Receptivity*, pp. 48-49, 97-101.
[12]See *Spiritual Direction*, pp. 20-23, 31-32.

formed being has reached completion (2 Co 4:16). Between inception and death there usually exist several critical thresholds together with their more or less prolonged stages of development.

Chapter 2

CRITICAL THRESHOLDS OF SPIRITUAL GENESIS

In an optimal situation, we distinguish seven critical thresholds of adult spiritual development, including individual creation and personal death. In every case of human existence, there must be at least two: coming into being and leaving this world.

A. Critical Thresholds

In the previous chapter we described in general terms the notion of threshold. Now we need to amplify that description in the context of "critical thresholds."

The term "critical" derives from the New Testament *krino*, meaning to separate, to make a distinction between, to exercise judgment upon. A person normally experiences many thresholds on diverse levels (physical, emotional, psychological, spiritual) in the course of life. However, not all thresholds are critical.

"Critical thresholds" designate those which are more fundamental: those which really separate one stage from another, those which delineate basic qualitative distinctions in progress and upon which solid judgments are made. Three qualities characterize critical thresholds: (1) They are radical. (2) They are irreversible. (3) They are successive.

(1) Critical thresholds are radical. They affect us down to our roots; every cell in our body, each attitude, value, principle, belief, conviction. The degree to which these critical thresholds affect us may not be immediately apparent. Nonetheless, the fact remains: We are radically changed, even if it takes us years to recognize the fact.

(2) We are also irreversibly changed, after having passed through a critical threshold. Initially, this irreversibility is relative, however. Until sufficient stability is achieved in the new stage of development, we may continue to experience a certain shifting back and forth between the two stages which the threshold separates. Such fluctuation is normal, since there remains a great deal of continuity between the latter phases of one stage and the initial phases of the next. Once greater stability is attained, our inner movement is towards the next stage and away from the one left behind.

(3) Furthermore, the previous critical threshold is ordinarily necessary before passing on to the next. God is certainly not limited in any way. Yet, he seldom jumps over or suspends a critical threshold. He may compress several together into a very short time span, but once they are begun in a certain succession he does not usually omit any. This truth will become apparent as we treat the critical thresholds of adult spiritual genesis in their optimal order.

A critical threshold may comprise any number of lesser thresholds. For example, in the area of personal accountability there are normally many breakthroughs on various levels (physical, emotional, psychological) which gradually converge during our adolescent years to prepare us for adult responsibility. These less critical thresholds, while remaining significant in their proper context, can nonetheless be sublimated, made up for in later life, interchanged with others, etc. These lesser breakthroughs lack the three qualities characteristic of the more critical ones.

The word "threshold" is itself a household word. It designates the sill of a doorway which divides one room from another. Applied to life's inner journey, threshold denotes a turning point, a crossroads, a breakthrough which, if pursued, launches the pilgrim into a new stage of faith, hope and love.

A critical threshold marks the point of intensity where the inner development of one stage of spiritual growth, having matured more fully, gives way to a new stage. In relation to the preceding one, this newly emerged stage is characterized by a more qualitative way of being, a more transformed manner of becoming. A critical threshold in spiritual genesis is comparable to that moment when a caterpillar becomes a butterfly or when water vaporizes.

A traumatic event in a person's life frequently precipitates the emergence of a threshold. Through a serious illness, a disruption in a personal relationship, failure in some major undertaking or the death of a loved one, spiritual growth which has been converging for quite some time may reach synthesis in an instant. The catalyst for the synthesis (or breakthrough) would be the trauma itself. Thus, what has been building up for many years can reach a threshold of development in and through a single event.

God is not limited to traumatic events, however. His transforming and purifying love can just as effectively bring us through our critical breakthroughs without such occurrences. In these cases, God draws us almost imperceptibly from one stage to another. Thresholds are integral to the process of spiritualization whether we advert to their taking place or not. In cases where God does not use a traumatic event as his instrument of transition, we may still experience the actual crossing of a given threshold as somewhat traumatic, since it is so radical and irreversible.

While each critical threshold remains unique, there are, nonetheless, three characteristics common to all those which occur between individual creation and personal death: restlessness, transition and stabilization.

(1) *Restlessness*: A certain interior disquiet or anxiousness begins to assert itself in our lives. We start losing the kind of meaningfulness which we had previously experienced. This perception coincides with a sense that something is lacking in our lives, despite all that we have and can

do. There is an urgency for something more, usually without being able to identify precisely what this "more" consists in. The initial stirrings of approaching a threshold can begin at an identifiable moment, or they can arise imperceptibly over a considerable period of time.

(2) *The Transition*: This is our passage out of the old mode of becoming into the new one. It is the movement from one stage of spiritual genesis to the next. This transition requires pulling up old roots, letting go familiar surroundings, reevaluating our identity, our values and our commitments. Certain things must be discarded, while others have to be realigned in view of the new intensity of life to which God is calling us.

The interior change which characterizes the crossing of a threshold affects all aspects of our lives. New attitudes, new values, renewed convictions must be translated into behavior. Some people seem to fluctuate at the point of passage, at least for a while. They go back and forth between their old mode and the new one. Thus, a person being drawn into contemplative prayer may still find discursive meditation helpful at times.

The passage through a threshold may in some instances transpire very quickly, in one fell swoop, as it were. In other cases the passage may take years, even decades. One person may make the transition in relative calm and peace, without undue disturbance or turmoil. Another may experience intense confusion, anxiety and fear in the course of a passage.

(3) *Stabilization*: Gradually we become at home in the mystery of our new life in God. We are content to have let go the past and are well immersed in the challenges of the present. Even as we grow accustomed to this new stage of transformed life, however, the Spirit is already leading us toward a progressively deeper quality of life in Christ and thus eventually to a more advanced threshold of spiritualization. Greater incorporation in Christ always lies further up ahead.

B. Varying Degrees of Criticalness

Obviously, not all seven critical thresholds of spiritual genesis are of equal criticalness. The passage from nonbeing to someone destined to eternal glory — the first threshold: individual creation — is both utterly incomparable and incomprehensible: "Oh, the depth of the riches, the wisdom and the knowledge of God! How inscrutable his judgments and unsearchable his ways" (Rm 11:33). Likewise the final threshold — our personal death, our actual passage from this life into eternity — is in a class all by itself: "The eye has not seen, the ear has not heard, it has not even so much as entered into the heart of anyone what God has prepared for those who love him" (1 Co 2:9).

Moreover, the five intervening adult critical thresholds —immersion in creation, emergence through creation, personal conversion, spiritual espousal and spiritual marriage — are not homogeneous either. The most critical of these five is emergence through creation. This is so because everything that precedes it is directed towards it, and the three thresholds which follow it constitute new intensities, greater radicalness and more pronounced irreversibility of the same basic emergence all the way through creation.

We must realize that we are dealing with an ever increasingly spiritual and qualitative entity: the transformation in God and by him of the whole human person.

Our individual creation is both instantaneous and ongoing. Creation is instantaneous in the sense that we and our time begin at a specific instant and in a particular place with all that we inherit. Our creation is also ongoing, since we are never complete until the act of death itself. Our personal death is the crowning act of our individual creation in time and space.

Dying is also both instantaneous and ongoing. Our final act of dying — our personal death — occurs at a precise time and place. Yet, we truly begin dying the very moment we come into being and we continue dying right up to death inclusive.

So, the process by which we are created and in which we die is contiguous with every instant and stage of our earthly sojourn. Moreover, the thresholds of immersion and emergence, together with personal conversion, spiritual espousal and spiritual marriage, are but specific critical breakthroughs of the same continuous process of transforming union.

Chapter 3

OVERVIEW OF THE SUCCESSIVE CRITICAL THRESHOLDS OF SPIRITUAL GENESIS

A twofold question may be posed: Why study the critical thresholds and stages of spiritual genesis at all? Would it not be an act of deeper faith to let God do with us what he wills, without trying to figure out where we are on our journey?

We respond: from one point of view, yes; from another perspective, no. If one is operating out of a static and quantitative mind-set, any attempt to discover "where one is" will prove futile and is contrary to growth in evangelical faith. However, for the real searcher, for the person with a sense of mystery and of the qualitative, such a quest proves invaluable. It is an exercise of one's faith seeking understanding.

On the one hand, there exists a craving to know which is part of our poverty and which remains antagonistic to faith development.[1] On the other hand, our spirit needs to understand something of its faith experience so that we can more consciously and more voluntarily give ourselves to God's transforming and purifying love.[2] If God had wanted us to receive him as a cup receives coffee, he would have made us

---

[1]See *Contemplation*, pp. 88-89; *Receptivity*, pp. 49-53, 97-101.
[2]See *Contemplation*, pp. 131-133.

out of glass or plastic. Obviously, that is not the case. It is his will that we receive him knowingly and willingly, responding to his initiative with love intensified by some understanding of what he is doing.

In line with the above response, an informed appreciation of the critical thresholds and stages of adult spiritual genesis, together with the principles required for their discernment, is of paramount importance for spiritual directors. Moreover, any serious pilgrim will benefit immensely from such a study, since the matter which we discuss eventually affects all of us one way or another. This study can help each person dissipate many illusions, and it can enhance his/her quest for God "by unknowing."

A. Schema of the Critical Thresholds

At this point in our discussion, it is useful to visualize in schematic form the critical thresholds of optimal adult interior development. Traditionally, Christian authors employ two basic metaphors to describe the transformation of a human person in Christ: deepening and ascending. For purposes of our schema, we choose the latter, since growth is more readily visualized as a process heading upward rather than proceeding downward. Thus, the schema is to be viewed from bottom to top.

Any schema possesses innate limitations. This schematic outline, however, is immeasurably more limited than others, since it attempts to summarize the ineffable mystery of God's dealings with each individual. We have never known anyone in whom God's transforming and purifying activity has proceeded in exactly the neat and orderly fashion which this schema portrays. Possibly there has never been such a person. Nonetheless, something of all this spiritual genesis applies to each of us more or less, one way or another, in God's own time. Moreover, it is helpful for our faith-understanding to have a frame of reference. Jesus himself occasionally used this type of pedagogical tool in his parables. For instance, the story of the farmer going out to sow

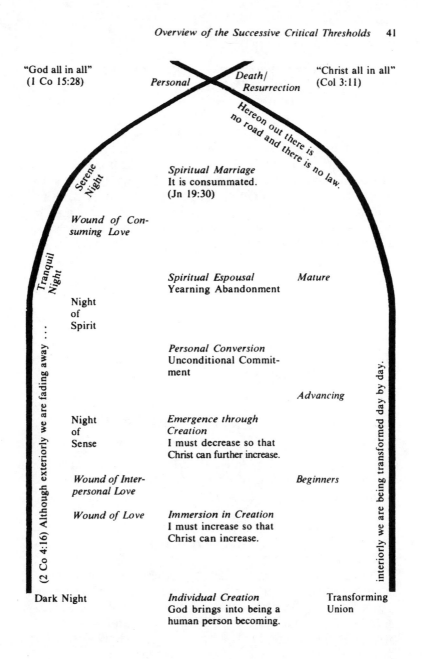

"God all in all"
(1 Co 15:28)

Personal

Death/ Resurrection

"Christ all in all"
(Col 3:11)

Hereon out there is
no road and there is no law.

Serene Night

Spiritual Marriage
It is consummated.
(Jn 19:30)

Wound of Consuming Love

Tranquil Night

Spiritual Espousal
Yearning Abandonment

Mature

Night
of
Spirit

Personal Conversion
Unconditional Commitment

Advancing

(2 Co 4:16) Although exteriorly we are fading away . . .

Night
of
Sense

Emergence through Creation
I must decrease so that Christ can further increase.

Wound of Interpersonal Love

Beginners

Wound of Love

Immersion in Creation
I must increase so that Christ can increase.

interiorly we are being transformed day by day.

Dark Night

Individual Creation
God brings into being a human person becoming.

Transforming Union

his seed describes various levels of listening and responding to God's word (Mt 13:3-23). Once we grasp the schema as a frame of reference, we then need to let it go so that we can continue our journey to the Father by faith.

The schema is called "optimal" because it unfolds under ideal conditions. Yet, each element of the schema emerges from authentic life-situations and helps us appreciate a little more explicitly the mystery of God's abiding love within us, together with our struggling response in love to him. When interpreted in the manner intended, this schema and its ensuing theological explanation will hopefully enhance our appreciation of mystery as mystery, rather than detract from it.

B. *Explanation of the Schema*

To prepare the reader for an in-depth study of each threshold and stage of adult spiritual genesis, we present first an overall explanation of our schema.

(1) INDIVIDUAL CREATION AND PERSONAL DEATH

The act of creation whereby God brings into being an individual human person so transcends our normal usage of the word "threshold" that we apply the term in this instance only in its most analogical sense. Yet, there is a kind of passage: that is, from nothing at all to someone destined to become one with All.

God directly and immediately creates each human person within the matter prepared by the co-creative activity of one's parents. For the rest of that individual's earthly sojourn, God continues to operate directly and immediately with him/her, until that person is completely formed in God's image (Gn 1:26; 2 Co. 3:18), until God has become all in him/her (1 Co 15:28; Col 3:11).

The direct and immediate activity of God within us constitutes the contemplative dimension of human life. This contemplative thrust intensifies progressively till death. Our final human act in dying is eminently a contemplative act: the unreserved abandonment of our whole self to God in faith and love. God works with us also mediately: through a myriad of influences both from within us and from outside us. In a sense all creation has a bearing on our spiritual development.

When God brings us into being — when we receive our initial act of existence — he creates us becoming: becoming who we are meant to be. We are truly human from the moment of inception, but we are not the complete human we are meant to become except in death.

Death is the culmination of our individual creation, at least as far as this mortal life is concerned. In death, our entire self is transformed in God. The whole person dies. The whole person is resurrected.[3] Death is the moment of maximum human consciousness, optimum freedom and final decision. Death is the threshold towards which all other thresholds tend.

Individual creation and personal death encompass the entirety of our earthly existence. On the one hand, death follows creation as an ending follows a beginning. But, on the other hand, both are concomitant from beginning to end. This side of the resurrection, there is never an instant in which we are not being created more in the image of God or in which we are not dying more to self. Concretely, our individual, ongoing creation (as well as re-creation) and our continuous dying are the two arms of God's all-embracing love for us. All other thresholds of spiritual genesis exist within that embrace. The point at which our being created and our dying coincide is our personal death/resurrection.

In God's initial act of creating us, we are not only brought into being becoming and given a participation in the universal call to holiness, but we are also empowered with a personal vocation. Who, how and what we are to become in

[3]See *Contemplation*, pp. 16-18; *Receptivity*, pp. 89-91, 97-103.

God are integrated into our individuality from our very beginning. We receive a personal identity at the moment of inception, but we are never all we are meant to be until death. What links our beginning with our completion is commonly called our "vocation": *how* we are to become who/what we are meant to be.

God not only gives each person a call to transformation in himself, but he also endows each one with a unique way of pursuing that universal vocation. These ways, though unique to each individual, fall into certain general lifestyles: marriage, celibacy, the single state, etc. Within these basic lifestyles there exists a variety of gifts and ministries: parenthood, priesthood, diaconate, education, management, etc. We tend to conceive all these ministries as vocations within our basic vocation to a particular way of life. We are also inclined to categorize these different types of vocation in straight lines. There are, of course, universally recognized exceptions to our straight-line conceptualizations. Occasionally, people do change careers. Some widows do enter religious life. Some priests and nuns obtain dispensations and marry.

God, however, is not bound by any of our categories or straight lines. An individual's vocation can zigzag through all our conceptualizations and defy our wildest attempts at creating order and logic in a given instance: "My ways are not your ways. My thoughts are not your thoughts. This is Yahweh who speaks" (Is 55:7-8).

Each person possesses a unique vocation in life. Even though at times certain aspects of that vocation fall within our human powers of conceptualization and categorization, we never fully realize — either existentially or intellectually — the full extent of our vocation except in death. We cannot comprehend in this life all the ways God uses us or all the intricacies of his cooperation with each of our yes's and no's. We cannot even begin to imagine how he converts everything to our good or to the good of all those he brings into our lives. God's working with us and in spite of us remains completely beyond us (Jn 5:17; Rm 11:33-36).

Our vocation is that to which God's love calls us here and now as well as ultimately. Our individual vocation evolves concretely from moment to moment, with each yes, no and maybe on our part.

Strictly speaking, no one ever loses his/her vocation. It can only be found. If we say "yes," God moves forward with us. If we resist, he breaks down our resistances until there remains nothing left but "yes." If we insist on "no," God continues to work with us in another direction until he gets us finally where he wants us. God does not change our vocation. He changes us.

Every vocation within the universal call to holiness is necessarily temporal, since it unfolds within the limitations of this mortal life. God never forces a vocation upon us. Sooner or later, one way or another we acquiesce willingly and irresistibly to it (Jer 1: 4-10; 20:7). Our vocation is a fire burning in our heart, imprisoned in our bones. We cannot frustrate it indefinitely (Jer 20:9).

Therefore, our vocation is not a *thing*. It is an integral, evolving part of our personhood. It is part of becoming our true self in God. Our unique vocation is the becoming aspect of our individual creation and personality carried forward into eternity. Our vocation is how we become fully ourselves in God. Death brings it all together. Death constitutes the ultimate convergence of all our becoming in God.

(2) IMMERSION IN AND EMERGENCE THROUGH CREATION

All human life between inception and death is characterized by this twofold rhythm: immersion in creation for Christ and emergence through creation with him. These are but two phases of a single movement: like breathing in and breathing out: like the arsis and thesis of a musical measure. "All the different shades of holiness are contained in the innumerable permutations of these two aspects of the

breath by which the soul lives: first taking its fill of possess-
ing things, and then sublimating them in God."⁴ That is the
breath of the true mystic.

In the normal course of human events, we must first
increase so that Christ can increase. We develop our talents.
We take advantage of the opportunities that come our way.
We build up as rich a personhood and as productive a life as
circumstances permit. In imitation of the Word Incarnate,
we plunge into creation, and there mingling with created
things "seize hold upon and disengage from them all that
they contain of life eternal, down to the very last fragment."⁵

In a certain sense, the complex of realities which comprise
what we call immersion span the whole of our mortal existence. They are present as long as we continue to breathe and
take nourishment. Yet, the stage of immersion remains most
noticeable at the initial phases of human development. As
we grow through infancy, childhood, adolescence and well
into adulthood, we see the dynamics of immersion most
operative.

For most of us, this interior threshold and stage — for it is
both — is so connatural that we rarely even advert to the
fact that it is taking place. Psychologically and physically,
immersion as a stage frequently covers the greater part of
our earthly sojourn: from birth to midlife. Optimally,
immersion as a specific interior threshold corresponds to
the psychological and spiritual awakenings of late adolescence and early adulthood.

As we mature in our immersion in creation, we become
more aware of God and of Christ as person as well as
intimate friend. Our prayer becomes more personal, more
conversational, more deliberately affective. Earlier, we may
have tended to be formal: "saying prayers" or reading some-
body else's prayers. Now, however, our prayer is our own as
we communicate spontaneously friend to friend. The quality of our work takes on an added dimension of intentional-
ity. There may have always been quality in our attitude and

⁴*Writings*, p. 261. See *Receptivity*, pp. 83-85; *Contemplation*, pp. 117-122.
⁵*Writings*, p. 222.

in the end product, but as the stage of immersion progresses this quality becomes more explicit in our minds. We specifically try to be quality-oriented both for ourselves and for others because of Christ.

The need for, as well as the practice of, self-discipline becomes increasingly apparent as we immerse ourselves in creation for Christ. Life is full of hard choices. Moreover, the need to rise above our immaturities is seen as the only qualitative way to embrace freedom and assume our personal responsibilities.

If we are true to life and to grace, we cannot continue indefinitely in the direction of full human development of our energies and talents. Gradually, and as a result of our immersion in creation, we become aware of the emergence of a new direction within us. This latter steadily grows more dominant and eventually reverses our previous impulse towards building up self. This new direction expresses itself as a predilection for detachment: I must decrease so that Christ may further increase both within me and around me (Jn 3:30).

The inevitable experience of human life is that we have hardly arrived at the zenith of our accomplishments when we are ready to leave them, retire and move on. Having taken our fill of the world and of ourselves, we discover one day that we are possessed by an intense need to die to self and to leave all self-interests behind. Moreover, for one faithful to life and grace this predilection for detachment is not the consequence of failure or of despair, but rather the normal development of effort and of success.

So begins the next threshold and stage of our formation in Christ Jesus: that of passing all the way through creation (or of emergence) with him.[6]

The major writings of St. John of the Cross presuppose that the reader has already passed through this threshold of emergence. Other spiritual authors — like St. Teresa of Jesus, St. Ignatius of Loyola, St. Francis de Sales — spend a great deal of time and effort trying to lead the soul through

[6]See *Writings*, pp. 222, 259-264; *Receptivity*, pp. 89-103, 106-109, 114-120.

the various spiritual phases of immersion, especially its latter phases. Teilhard de Chardin treats the gist of the threshold of immersion under the titles: *Divinization of Our Activities* and *The Passivities of Growth.* He capsulizes the sense of emergence when speaking of *The Passivities of Diminishment* and our *Receptivity of a Superior Order.*[7]

We speak of the threshold of emergence through creation with Christ as having been crossed once the pilgrim is acutely aware of its predominance in his/her life. As such, the crossing of this threshold may take years, even decades. Moreover, once begun, emergence only intensifies with the passage of time, until death which is its apex. The other critical thresholds of adult spiritual genesis — personal conversion, spiritual espousal and spiritual marriage — are further radical intensifications of emergence.

Personal conversion is a special modality of emergence. It is a singular moment in our lives. Emergence and personal conversion go together like two sides of the same coin. "Emergence" denotes not only a threshold but also an élan which endures for the rest of our lives. "Personal conversion," on the other hand, designates a unique instant of breakthrough and definitive stabilization in the process of emergence. From that moment on, we realize that we are possessed by Christ and that we wholeheartedly desire to surrender ourselves to him in love, hope and faith.

Spiritual espousal is a radical intensification of our conversion to God in terms of an insatiable yearning for complete union with him. We abandon ourselves to our Beloved as lovers do in their betrothal. This yearning is crowned by *spiritual marriage* wherein the soul experiences the most intimate communion with God that is possible this side of the resurrection. This last threshold never occurs long before death, since our mortal existence cannot sustain for very long the overwhelming force of this divine intimacy.

The threshold of emergence marks the beginning of contemplation as well as the night of sense, although vestiges of both were already present in the latter phases of immersion.

---

[7]See *D. Milieu*, pp. 49-111; *Receptivity*, pp. 83-123.

From then on, we experience God not only as friend, but specifically as Beloved. We not only love him, but we are specifically in love with him. We say "in love" not in the emotional sense of infatuation (of falling in and out of love), but in the mystical sense of definitive immersion in God, of mutual indwelling (Jn 15:4-5), of radical faith in Father, Son and Spirit. Despite all our limitation, resistance and hesitation, we enter more and more voluntarily into a deepening relationship in faith, hope and love with the Trinity.

Over the course of a lifetime an individual's personal prayer passes through several successive stages of development. Each stage is characterized by a particular kind of subjective consciousness, which itself reflects something of God's intense activity within the person at a given time.

First, praying is ordinarily perceived as a "should": I ought to say grace before meals; I should say my Rosary; I ought to go to Mass on appointed days; etc. Some degree of guilt is frequently the emotional response for omitting one or other of those prescriptions. Some people, however, experience considerable relief—a newfound freedom—after abandoning that system of do's and don't's, whether in whole or in part.

A second intensity of experiencing prayer is associated with the stage of immersion. Here praying is often a pleasure, an exuberance, an uplifting sensation which calls me back for more and more. I really like praying. Prayer is fun. I look forward to it as I would an enjoyable visit with a close friend.

This sensation, however, does not last indefinitely. It inevitably gives way to aridity. Prayer can then seem like a drudgery, a chore. The more we try, the less we feel of God, of anyone or anything. Praying can even become downright distasteful. Often we are sorely tempted to abandon it for something that appears useful or that is tangibly meaningful. Many people give up personal prayer altogether at this time, especially if they persist in this state for several years or decades.

A final intensity of praying—one which in fact never ends, but only progresses with maturity—is prayer as a need: I hunger after prayer and solitude. I thirst for more spiritual intimacy with my Beloved. Paradoxically, this final stage dawns for some only after they have in fact abandoned praying for some time and perhaps have even tried to abandon God himself (Jer 20:9). It is as if their waywardness finally caught up with them and turned them completely around (Lk 15:17). Their very narcissism brought them to their knees. Interiorly they have come full circle. At first, they may have prayed because they thought they were supposed to do so. They were led by imposed law or by conscience. Now, however, they pray because they need to interiorly. They have to pray, just as they have to eat and breathe and sleep. They cannot make it through the day without some serious prayer. This is the experience of a person maturing in contemplation.

(3) TRANSFORMING UNION AND THE DARK NIGHT

The schema of the critical thresholds represents the fullest possible life in Christ this side of the resurrection. Each person passes through all of it, at least qualitatively in death.

On the side of the transforming union, St. John of the Cross employs three terms to indicate the level of interior progress characteristic of persons undergoing God.[8] "Beginners" (*principiantes*). These are the ones being initiated by God into the deeper realms of mystery and faith: the beginning of contemplation. "Advancing" (*aprovechados*). These are the improved ones; those well on their way in the process of divinization; those profiting from the activity of God within them. "Mature" (*perfectos*). These are the tried and tested ones, faithful and fully committed. These are being prepared for the final leap into eternity.

On the side of the dark night — which is caused directly by the intensity of God's transformation of us in himself[9] —John uses three words to describe the wounds which are

---

[8]See *Ascent*, I, 1, 3; *Night*, II, 20, 4.
[9]See *Receptivity*, pp. 48-49.

produced by the gradual intensification of our love for God.[10] "Wound of love" (*herida*). This refers to a general aching for God as he is experienced in and through his creation. "Wound of interpersonal love" (*llaga*). Our love of human persons adds a new and intensified quality to our encounter with God in and through his creation. We not only experience him in *things*, but especially in *people*. Thus, the created has opened our heart undeniably to the Uncreated. The finite has led us beyond itself to the Infinite.[11] "Wound of consuming love" (*cauterio*). This cauterization results from the force of the Living Flame of Love within us — the Holy Spirit. The previous two wounds were caused by God both directly and through the medium of creatures, but stressing the role of the latter. The wound of consuming love, on the other hand, derives almost entirely from the direct and immediate activity of God within us, with relatively little mediation of creatures. Thus, God himself readies us for our definitive abandonment to him in death.

John of the Cross distinguishes four phases of the one dark night of the soul. The night of sense can be compared to the darkness following sunset. This progresses to midnight and beyond for several more hours: the night of spirit. The tranquil night is likened to the very first glimmers of predawn. The serene night is dawn just before sunrise. Personal death, of course, is the full light of day.

In his *Sketch of Mount Carmel*,[12] John of the Cross depicts three paths up the mountain. The one to the left —the way of the "goods of heaven" — reaches a dead end with this observation: "The more I desired to possess them, the less I had. Now that I no longer desire them, I have them all without desire." The path to the right — the way of the "goods of earth" — also reaches an impasse with this note: "The more I desired to seek them, the less I found. Now, to

---

[10]See *Canticle*, stanzas 1 and 7; *Flame*, stanza 2.

[11]See *Receptivity*, pp. 18-31.

[12]See K. Kavanaugh and O. Rodriguez, trans., *The Collected Works of St. John of the Cross*, (ICS, 1983) pp. 66-67.

the degree that I desire them less, I have them all without desire." The third path — the straight and narrow one up the middle — is the way *nada*: "nothing, nothing, nothing and even on the Mount nothing." But this way of *nada* does not go all the way up the mountain. It peters out about half way to the top. Then, near the summit where one would have expected the straight and narrow path to have continued, John writes: "Here on out there is no road, because for the just person there is no law. S/he is a law unto him/herself."

Finally, in our personal death-resurrection Father, Son and Spirit are our *Todo*, our All: "God all in all" (1 Co 15:28); "Christ all in all" (Col 3:11).

THRESHOLD AND STAGE OF IMMERSION

Chapter 4

IMMERSION IN CREATION FOR CHRIST

Our immersion in created matter begins quite literally in the womb and endures into the tomb. Even in the resurrection, the transformed human person retains an essential link with physical creation.

In this chapter, however, we do not treat the dynamics of immersion from our initial breath till our last. Rather, we examine immersion as a specific — indeed, the first — critical threshold and stage of adult spiritual genesis. As such, immersion designates that point of our inner journey where we consciously begin to develop a personal relationship with Father, Son and Spirit. We explicitly seek to let God become the center of our lives.

A. Immersion

As a particular threshold, immersion marks the passage from a primarily externalized value system to a more interiorized one. Prior to this threshold, we had been introduced to a faith life through the teaching and example of our parents, family and local Christian community (Rm 10:14-17). We practiced our faith by participating at Mass, saying the rosary and other prayers, making the first Fridays, donating to worthy causes, performing charitable deeds. In all this, however, our primary motivation was linked to the fact that others had told us that these practices were good and meaningful. These were the things to do, because significant others said they were important. We had not yet reached the point of personal incorporation of these same attitudes.

Before reaching the threshold of immersion, some people live in apparent indifference to God; others in outright rejection or denial of him. These have limited and sometimes warped exposure to the living witness of the faith community. They may even reject this witness as unmeaningful or hypocritical.

But somewhere along the line something happens. It may be a chance encounter or a traumatic event, like a death in the family. It may be a gradual awakening or a sudden turnaround. Whatever the catalyst and however long it takes to effect, we come to a new realization. Our attitudes start changing and we begin to encounter Christ as person. Moreover, we become aware of a desire to foster an intimate, loving relationship with him. A genuine friendship with God is engendered.

The integral mystery of the incarnation is this: The Father sends his Son into the world (Jn 3:16). The eternal Word plunges into created things to the point of becoming flesh and dwelling among us (Jn 1:14). He becomes exactly like us in all things except sin (Ph 2:7; 2 Co 13:4; Heb 4:15). Having immersed himself in creation, he passes all the way through, returning to the Father (Jn 13:1). In returning to the Father he draws the whole of creation to himself (Jn 12:32), recapitulating all in himself (Col 1:15-20).

The threshold of immersion is, therefore, our awakening to this mystery as something unmistakably personal. Christ not only died for all. He died specifically for me. The course of our lives is forever changed by this realization. Ideally speaking, the sacramental celebration of this crossroads on our journey is Confirmation.

The grace of Confirmation is directly linked to our ability to personally confirm and to voluntarily incorporate what was begun without our conscious awareness in Baptism. In

Baptism we celebrated sacramentally our birth into human-kind, our rebirth in terms of divine adoption and our formal entrance into the institutional Church. Confirmation is the culminating phase of that prior initiation. By Confirmation, we personally own and ratify all the years of physical, intellectual, emotional and spiritual growth which has brought us to this first threshold and stage of interior adulthood.

To confer the sacrament of Confirmation prior to the passage of immersion is to cheat the young Christian of a very important dimension of this threshold and of his/her voluntary incorporation in Christ. Most people need to celebrate this breakthrough somehow: either sacramentally or parasacramentally. If Confimation has already been administered at an earlier, less meaningful stage of develop-ment, some substitute has to be found to mark this passage. In our day, practices like Baptism in the Spirit often serve this purpose.

Once we have crossed the threshold of our initial exper-ience of a personal God, the basic principle of development in the ensuing stage of interior growth is that of building up a strong self for Christ: I must increase so that he can increase in me and all around me.

The soul who wishes to belong firmly to Christ must prepare in itself an abundant matter to sanctify, a rich nature. As confirmed Christians, our first duty both to ourselves and to others is to develop a vigorous self for Christ through the use of creatures. Our first care "must be to extend by human effort in every direction that leads to Spirit the still unfinished work of visible creation."[1]

This is necessary because "each of our works by its more or less remote or direct effect upon the spiritual world, contributes to the perfection of Christ in his mystical total-ity. . . . By my activity, I adhere to the creative power of God. I coincide with it. I become not only its instrument but also its living prolongation. . . . Each increase that I bestow

[1] *Writings*, p. 260.

upon myself or upon created things is translated into some increase in my power to love and some progress in the blessed hold of Christ upon the Universe.... God is inexhaustibly attainable in the totality of our action."[2]

Therefore, without hesitation and in a responsible manner our first stage of evolution in Christ is that of plunging into created things. We actualize our capabilities. We use our gifts. We exercise our talents. We thus broaden our understanding, strengthen our will, arouse our enthusiasm to love.

But we are weak. We are sinners. Our involvement in creation is accompanied inevitably by some engrossment and inordinate attachment. These eventually have to go. Yet, these immaturities do not negate the importance of a thorough immersion into God's world and ours, since the prime focus of this threshold remains the building up of the Body of Christ. It is basically God whom we pursue through the reality of created things. Our interest is indeed in creatures, but in such a way that we maintain a conscious dependence upon God's presence in them. "Within ourselves and our individual development, it is not precisely ourselves that we seek but rather One greater than ourselves. We seek him to whom we know that we are destined."[3]

This initial stage of spiritualization imposes upon us the work of development for God. This growth affects the whole person on every level: physical, intellectual, emotional, spiritual. This development is accomplished in and through our involvement both with inanimate things and with persons. Through our human endeavors and personal relationships, God wounds us with his love. The "wound of love" which St. John of the Cross describes in *Canticle* 1-7 is the necessary result of mature immersion in creation. Essentially, it consists in the realization that no matter how wonderful, helpful, meaningful a given creature is in our lives, that creature is still not God in himself. The creature

[2]*D. Milieu*, pp. 62-63.
[3]*D. Milieu*, p. 73.

thus opens us to the Uncreated.[4] This wound of love increases throughout the stage of immersion and becomes a major factor in the threshold of emergence.

While the threshold of immersion can occur earlier, it is frequently crossed somewhere in late adolescence. The ensuing stage of immersion then extends well into adulthood. However, since there are so many late bloomers, sometimes this breakthrough does not happen until much later. It may even occur so late in life that there is no time left for a stage as such to develop.

B. Passage through the Stage of Immersion

During the stage of immersion, the building up of a strong self for Christ generally comprises three broad consecutive phases: (1) the discovery and establishment of our individuality, (2) the development of a sense of vocation, and (3) the reevaluation of our achievements and choices.

(1) THE DISCOVERY AND ESTABLISHMENT OF OUR INDIVIDUALITY

We discover and establish our individuality in many ways: for instance, by developing personal friendships with our peers both male and female, by exploring our sexual identity, by forming a world view (which is initially quite idealistic), by continuing our education, by searching for a career or profession, by becoming emancipated from our family, by discovering latent talents, by beginning to respect differences in other persons' viewpoints, and by learning to communicate effectively.

The Myers-Briggs Personality Type Indicator and similar psychological inventories can be of invaluable assistance in helping us to identify our individual temperaments and personality profiles. These psychological tools can also

[4]See *Receptivity*, pp. 23-31.

facilitate recognition of both our strengths and our shadowy sides.

(2) THE DEVELOPMENT OF A SENSE OF VOCATION

Most of us have far more talents than we can possibly pursue in a single lifetime. As we pass through the stage of immersion, we are drawn inexorably from within to narrow down our options and to make some hard choices. Oftentimes without our realizing it, a sense of particular vocation begins to impress itself upon our consciousness, and we make our decisions accordingly. This sense of vocation develops into a general appreciation not only of who we are to become, but also of how and what we are to contribute to the building up of Christ.

Closely associated with a budding sense of vocation is the awakening of the potential to listen to oneself, to others and to God. The need to listen to God within us eventually brings us to an initial discovery of solitude. We need to go apart on occasion into silence and solitude to commune with God at the heart of all that is transpiring in our lives.

Life furnishes ample opportunity for the intensification of this capacity to listen. The deepening of intimate friendships, the experience of falling in love, the pain of being jilted in love, competition with others in work or sports, cooperation in team efforts, sharing a sense of solidarity with a particular group — all these force us to listen to others, to ourselves and to God.[5]

A keener sense of vocation and an increased ability to listen bring us to the awareness of a call to a particular way of life: married, single, celibate, for example. This realization normally takes years to develop and to test adequately. Far too many people jump into permanent commitments without sufficient extensive (time) and intensive (depth) discernment.

[5]See *Spiritual Direction*, pp. 51-66, 83-94, 119-160, 181-192.

An awakening sense of vocation necessarily opens us to the beginning of lifelong commitments. While certain life directions are being established, we have to continue, however, to remain disposed to modify our choices and commitments in response to changing circumstances and further experience of God within ourselves and within our world.

(3) REEVALUATION OF OUR ACHIEVEMENTS AND CHOICES

No sooner do we begin attaining our goals, establishing our priorities and living our commitments than we start reassessing these same accomplishments and decisions. The experience of not being completely satisfied with what we have thus far achieved for Christ triggers this reevaluation.[6] There is a nagging sense that something is lacking. We see that something more is necessary: We must die to self and to the world. This realization will inevitably blossom into the threshold of emergence where we must decrease so that Christ can further increase both within us and all around us (Jn 3:30).

6See *Receptivity*, pp. 27-31, 66-69.

Chapter 5

DISCERNMENT RELATED TO OUR IMMERSION IN CREATION

What signs indicate that we are successfully passing through the threshold and stage of immersion?

These signs or principles of discernment are basically four: (A) We actually involve ourselves in creation. We do not withdraw from it. (B) We search for God in and through his creation. We do not merely drift aimlessly in some direction. (C) We move from an idealistic to a realistic outlook on life. And (D) the contemplative element of our prayer life gradually asserts itself upon our consciousness. (This last principle will be treated in chapters 6 and 7.)

A. Involvement in Creation

Persons honestly searching for God seek him initially in and through the created. Their actual involvement in God's creation provides the nourishment for building up a strong self for Christ. By "creation" we mean both individual creatures (particular persons and things) as well as collective evolution. It behooves the spiritual director to help directees at this stage of development to discern whether they are seeking God through immersion in creation or whether they are basically attempting to journey to the Father by circumventing mature involvement.

Virtually everyone experiences tendencies towards both involvement in and withdrawal from creation, with one or the other thrust dominating. In the following paragraphs we contrast those persons who are principally inclined towards involvement with those whose dominant tendency is towards circumvention of creation.

Persons involved in creation tend to form intimate friendships, to be socially well-adjusted and capable of cooperation with others in team efforts, whether in work or in recreation. Withdrawn persons, on the other hand, have few or no intimate friends. They experience difficulty sustaining relationships. Problems in communicating with others pose considerable strain in group activities. Usually, withdrawn persons shun socializing and tend to be loners. These people try to go to God by cutting themselves off from the world, by abstaining from or avoiding the very things that are necessary for growth at this time.

Involved persons possess at least a rudimentary awareness that their activity contributes something towards a better world. All positive human endeavor —study, manual labor, service to others, research, etc. — has an altruistic meaning when seen in relation to God. Involved persons sense that what they do increases in some infinitesimal way Christ's hold on the universe. They have a conviction that they are really coworkers with God, even if the good results of their efforts escape their immediate notice.

Quite the contrary are withdrawn, egocentric persons. They usually view their activity as a job to get over and done with. Their prime remuneration is money, prestige or power. They are oriented not so much towards quality as towards personal gain. God can certainly use their activity to produce much quality. However, he accomplishes this in spite of them.

Both good intention (*operatio*) and as good an end result as we can produce (*opus*) are equally necessary for the confirmed Christian.[1] One without the other is halfhearted.

---

[1] See *D. Milieu*, pp. 49-70.

The gospel is diametrically opposed to any form of mediocrity or complacency (Lk 12:49-50).

Christians who are involved with creation possess a real love for the world and a healthy zest for life. They enjoy their interaction with people and things. Those trying to circumvent creation, on the other hand, frequently deny themselves pleasure and enjoyment. When pleasure is experienced, they tend to feel guilty or anxious. They are inclined to cut off a whole segment of the creation which God wants to use in their transformation. Christian asceticism and self-discipline are always necessary, but only within proper limits.[2] These isolationists approach life as if it were a host of functions, duties and obligations.

Involved persons are basically other-oriented. They can transcend their own likes and dislikes for the good of others. They allow Christ to become more and more the center of their life. Those circumventing creation, on the other hand, are caught up in self. They withdraw from Christian involvement. They are narcissistic and egotistical. As long as withdrawal persists, they remain locked in immaturity, denying themselves the very challenges necessary for growth in this first stage of adult spiritual genesis.

Christian involvement is, however, distinct from engrossment. Involvement consists in a twofold movement of attachment and detachment. Out of love for the world we plunge into created realities, while at the same time passing through them. After the example of Jesus, we do not stop along the way. Our detachment consists not in withdrawing from creation, but rather in continuing our involvement all the way through creation to the goal: eternal life in God.[3] This twofold movement of attachment and detachment is represented in the baptismal symbol of immersion and emergence, which Confirmation crowns.

In straining forward to God in and through creation, we leave behind something of ourselves and of creation. We pass through the created to find God at the heart of our-

[2]See *Contemplation*, pp. 110-115; *Receptivity*, pp. 44-48.
[3]See *Receptivity*, pp. 17-31, 114-120.

selves and of the universe. Engrossment occurs when we become fixated on some creature. We stop at the created as an end in itself instead of allowing it to point us beyond ourselves and itself. We make the created person or object into a god, and try to eke out of it what only God himself can bestow.

Involved Christians exhibit a willingness to take risk: the risk that is part of a vibrant faith. When the Spirit so indicates, they are ready to leave behind what is secure, familiar and certain in order to journey into the new and unknown. In contrast, isolationists tend to hang on for dear life. They will not let go their petty securities or familiar surroundings. For example, they cling to a particular method of prayer; to ministry exercised exclusively within a structured or institutional setting; to excessive attachment to family; to blind acceptance of authority. In effect, they try to shelter themselves from growth by wrapping themselves up in an imaginary cocoon.

The difference between involved persons and withdrawn persons exhibits itself also in their respective approaches to discernment. The maturely involved are open to God speaking through the created: through their intuition and common sense, through the legitimate authorities in their lives, through friends as well as through adversaries, through their activities and all that they undergo, through the myriad of concrete situations in which they are daily immersed. On the contrary, those circumventing creation lack this quality of openness and tend to put all kinds of restrictions on the manner in which God can speak. They imagine that they have a direct line to God. They claim that he reveals himself to them only by direct intervention. They stubbornly refuse to accept input or challenge from anyone else. Demanding of themselves and of others rigid adherence to the letter of the law, they remain oblivious to its spirit.

There is also considerable difference between the solitude of involved persons and the loneliness of persons circumventing creation. Involved persons seek out solitude as integral to their zest for life. The desire to be alone springs from a desire to drink at life's source. True solitude means remaining alone in loving community with Father, Son and Spirit. It means also being in communion with all creation in God. However, persons circumventing creation desire to be left alone in order to remain isolated. Their aloneness is a withdrawal from, rather than a being with, All. It is a retirement from life rather than an attempt to plumb the depths of life.[4]

In short, the person immersed in creation is one who is living life as fully as God wants, while the person circumventing creation is the casual observer standing on life's fringes.

B. Searching for God in and through Creation

During the stage of immersion, the spiritual director must also help directees discern whether they are truly seeking God (through involvement) or whether they are drifting aimlessly. There exist within most people tendencies towards both searching and drifting, with one or the other thrust dominating. We contrast the characteristics of those persons who are primarily searching with those who are basically drifting.

The question of whether persons are predominately searching or drifting can be difficult to discern accurately, since a certain experience of lostness is normal at this stage. Thus, the director has to view the directee's life over a considerable period of time. This overview is usually accomplished either by knowing the directee for several years or by going through the directee's life history.

Three broad, consecutive phases characterize our quest for God through creation during the stage of immersion. They are divergence, convergence and emergence. (This last phase should not be confounded with the next critical threshold which is emergence through creation with Christ.)

The first question that we ask ourselves as we cross the initial threshold of adult spiritual genesis is this: What does

4See *Contemplation*, pp. 97-99.

God want of me? Trying to respond, we branch out in a variety of directions. We have to test the waters. We explore the possibilities that lie open before us in order to discover which ones are compatible with our innermost being. These will be the pursuits which we experience as personally fulfilling and as meaningful for others. As we explore these divergent possibilities, we go down many blind alleys. We hit a lot of dead ends. We make mistakes. In order to find out who we are, we must first discover who we are not. In order to find our way, we need to discover what is not our way. Generally, a person passing through this phase of divergence experiences many mixed emotions: eagerness, enthusiasm and excitement together with confusion, lostness and ambivalence.

Much trial and error lead us to realize intuitively that only certain directions are compatible with our inner self. Gradually, the initial myriad of possibilities is narrowed down. For instance, a boy realizes that there are specific qualities that he wants in the girl whom he will someday marry. A young woman realizes that only certain professions are appealing to her in view of her values and priorities. In this convergence upon particular options, our self-identity continues to develop. We become more explicitly aware of the kind of lifestyle that is expressive of our inner self. Yet, confusion and ambivalence linger. This is normal.

The forces of convergence intensify to the point where emergence is finally reached. A compelling self-identity in God emerges. At this point we usually make a definite choice of lifestyle and of ministry in response of God's call. These fruits of our quest do not fully ripen, however, until we have crossed the next critical threshold of our spiritual genesis.

Thus, the true pilgrim passes through the dialectic of divergence, convergence and emergence. Despite much confusion and ambivalence, a positive movement forward is discernible. A certain clarity and refinement have emerged. This is in marked contrast to the drifter who shifts aimlessly and haphazardly every which way. This person has no basic sense of direction.

In the case of drifters, the first responsibility of the spiritual director is to help these persons become aware of their situation. Drifters are stuck in the phase of divergence. There exists a lack of emotional or personality development which prevents them from advancing. A classical example of this type is the "Don Juan": an individual who enters upon numerous passing relationships, but is incapable of sustaining any of them.

When dealing with true pilgrims, the director should discern in a general way where these directees are in the dialectic of divergence, convergence and emergence. This discovery helps directees appreciate that their experience is normal for a given phase (e.g. anxiety and uncertainty in the phase of divergence). They are thus encouraged to undergo their quest for God with patience and hope. The director should help these directees see that their pain and suffering are integral to authentic searching. Directors need also to take care that their directees do not make choices or commitments precipitously, or lock themselves into a particular phase when it is time to move on to the next.

Should the director-directee relationship be of short duration, spiritual direction will probably be confined to only one phase of the overall process of divergence, convergence and emergence. In this instance, the director does not try to accelerate the dialectic. Directors need to patiently accept their directees wherever they are in their quest for God. Directors afford whatever assistance is possible, but beyond that they have to trust God to meet their directees' needs elsewhere and through other means. Each one of these phases can take years to transverse.

Drifters are frequently lazy and undisciplined. They are like reeds swaying in the breeze. They are tossed to and fro by their whims and fancies. They shift narcissistically up and down the scale of their own likes and dislikes. They will not do anything that they do not *feel* like doing. Operating out of a basic sense of faith, responsibility or conviction is foreign to them.

Even in the midst of chaos and turmoil true searchers

remain disciplined and creative. In the process of convergence pilgrims have to eliminate many possible options in order to intensify a given direction. The source of these decisions is interior conviction coupled with an intuition enlightened by faith. They see that a certain choice is what God wants as well as what they really want, whether they like it or not.

Perseverance complements self-discipline, and is another sign of authentic searching. Drifters give up easily. They tend to abandon their task or direction before its time, especially when confronted with challenges or monotony. Perseverance denotes fidelity. It witnesses to that sustained effort and constancy necessary to see a work through to its end. In the spiritual life, this consistency comes from God, not from self. It requires a dying to self. Perseverance is the strength by which the Spirit enables us to go on doing what we are given to do by God.

A further authenticating sign of real searching is a certain spiritual anxiety. At first sight this truth may seem strange. Most people assume that the deeper a person searches for God, the more sure and tranquil his/her interior disposition should become. However, such is not the case, at least in the stage of immersion. The pilgrim is being drawn into deeper mystery and consequently farther away from his/her previous world of familiar surroundings. The pilgrim is beginning to travel more by dark faith than by precise standards. And this can be frightening at times. A certain anxiety is normal and healthy, since only the true searcher is worried about possibly making a mistake. The drifter could not care less.[5]

Furthermore, serious pilgrims look for guidance from others. They seek out and listen to the help that God makes available to them. Drifters cannot afford to accept spiritual direction, since to do so would necessarily put them on a definite course of action.

Drifters refuse to accept personal responsibility either for

[5]See *Contemplation*, pp. 65-68.

their own lives or for their choices. They are passive in the wrong sense. Often, they say: "Let God take care of things." However, they really mean: "Let whim and chance prevail." They are not passive in the mystical sense; that is, receptive and submissive to God. Rather, their passivity is towards their own inertness. In reality, they are scared to death of God, because they know that his providence costs too much. Drifters decide not to decide.

Pilgrims, in contrast, accept responsibility. They are open to God in all life's situations. They trust in God's providence and depend on him. In this context, true pilgrims exert initiative and creativity in actively seeking out and testing possible directions. They successfully balance receptivity (letting God's will be done) with activity (doing God's will).

Questioning oneself and others is another necessary element in authentic searching. Drifters tend to accept everything indiscriminately. They comply blindly to rules, laws and regulations, even when these serve no positive function. Drifters go through endless routines and all sorts of external practices simply because they think everyone else is doing the same. In fact, it may not cross the drifter's mind to ask whether or not such things are personally meaningful, just or even from God.

Searchers, on the other hand, entertain serious questions. These questions arise from discernment rather than from doubt, for it is not every spirit that we can trust (1 Jn 4:1). These questions are not posed in order to arrive at clear-cut answers. Instead, their purpose is to clear away debris and thus enable pilgrims to search more deeply into God's mysterious ways. More often than not God responds to this questioning with silence. It is not a dead silence, however, but one charged with presence, love and invitation to go further. Growth in evangelical faith requires intense questioning and pondering of the mysteries of salvation.[6]

Immersion in creation draws pilgrims to an awareness of a need for personal prayer and more solitude. Prior to this threshold the occasional "saying of prayers" had sufficed:

---

[6]See *Contemplation*, pp. 131-133.

grace before family meals, Mass on most Sundays, an aspiration to St. Anthony when the keys are lost. But now, true pilgrims need to commune with God on a more habitual basis. They need to pray the scriptures, meditate on the life of Christ, think about God in their own words. And all this means being alone with God more often: a "visit" in a quiet chapel somewhere, a solitary stroll in the woods or along the beach, turning off the TV and stereo for a while in order to enter into solitude.

Beyond a certain point, to drift is really to avoid God and personal responsibility. Drifting then means regressing. If such persons come for spiritual direction, directors need to take a careful look at the causes of such immaturity. Frequently, those causes lie in unresolved emotional and psychological disturbances. Thus, such persons may need a great deal of counseling or therapy or just growing up before spiritual direction can be realistically approached.

C. Transition from Idealism to Realism

As we cross the threshold of immersion in creation for Christ, we normally tend to be idealistic. We burn with enthusiasm to make a better world. We have numerous goals that we set out to achieve. Yet, as healthy as such an attitude is initially, progress through the stage of immersion is characterized by a gradual transition from idealism to realism. Spiritual directors are called upon to facilitate and encourage this movement. They need to be alert to any fixation which prevents the directee from progressing in this direction.

This idealism manifests itself in a variety of ways. Some people remain simplistic in their judgment. A thing is either absolutely right or wrong regardless of circumstances. Others think that their way of doing a certain thing is the only way. They believe that they have all the right answers to solve every difficulty. Still others expect immediate perfection of themselves and flawless virtue from those with whom they live or work.

No sooner have we plunged into creation, however, than idealism begins to clash with life. We begin to experience that the complexities and ambiguities of life do not fit into our simplistic outlook.

There are basically three awakenings which constitute indications of maturation from idealism to realism: (1) poverty of spirit, (2) the uniqueness of each individual, and (3) the mysteriousness of God.

(1) POVERTY OF SPIRIT

In the course of seeking God in creation, we are given our first bitter dose of poverty of spirit. If it has not already happened, we now have to face the truth of ourselves together with the agonizing limitations of our creatureliness and mortality. For an athlete, this may consist in losing the championship. For a laborer or executive, this may mean an indefinite layoff; for a parent, the loss or near loss of a child; for a religious, a major confrontation with a superior. Thus, during the stage of immersion we not only discover our God-given talents, strengths and gifts, but we also begin to experience in a more wrenching way sinfulness and limitations of all kinds. This causes us to move towards either cynicism or realism. Cynics tend to isolate themselves within their thwarted ideals. Realists let go their idealism, while continuing to pursue their ideal as best they can. The prayer of Alcoholics Anonymous captures aptly the sense of this transition: Lord, grant me the serenity to accept the things I cannot change; the courage to change the things I can; and the wisdom to know the difference.

Resolving the crisis of idealism means coming to a basic acceptance of ourselves and of others not only in their beauty and strength but especially in their failures and limitations. As we gravitate towards a more realistic attitude, we develop the essential Christian virtues of patience, tolerance and sympathy. We become compassionate, forgiving and gentle.

Those who remain fixated in idealism, however, display attitudes which are quite contrary. They cannot accept or integrate personal failure. In the experience of their own weakness, they are often harshly unforgiving towards themselves. They doubt God's merciful love for them. Faced with the poverty of others, they tend to be self-righteous, judgmental, uncompassionate and unforgiving. In a word: cynical.

(2) THE UNIQUENESS OF EACH INDIVIDUAL

Another sign of our movement towards realism is our increasing recognition of the fact that other persons are truly different from ourselves. Each person is wholly unique. Idealists tend to look upon significant people in their lives as other selves, as extensions of themselves. Tremendously unrealistic expectations are engendered in this context.

The acceptance of the other as basically different from ourselves has a twofold effect within us. First, the recognition of the otherness of each individual is a means through which we discover our own personal solitude. Second, it establishes also the basis for deep, intimate encounters with God through human friendships. For in accepting the uniqueness of others, we are less likely to become engrossed in them.

The discovery that others are truly different usually occurs through the painful shattering of illusions and false expectations. There is no more effective source of this stripping than the nitty-gritty of everyday life. When we refuse to let go our idealism at the appropriate time, we drift into isolation and thereby deny the solitary element of our lives. We demand that others be like ourselves and conform to our ways. When they do not, we reject them and sever our relationship with them. In so doing, we reject also the possibility of encountering God in them.

(3) THE MYSTERIOUSNESS OF GOD

Initially, our idealism had caused us to assume that we knew exactly who God is and where we were heading. As the bubbles burst, however, we become increasingly aware that God himself transcends anything we can think, imagine or feel him to be. A sense emerges that no matter how deeply we have experienced God thus far, he is infinitely beyond our grasp. Thus, we are forced to let go our naive or simplistic notions of who God is and where he is taking us. The words of Yahweh become starkly real: "My thoughts are not your thoughts. My ways are not your ways" (Is 55:8).

Chapter 6

DISCURSIVE PRAYER

Discursive prayer is the prayer form most characteristic of the threshold and stage of immersion. The adjective "discursive" comes from a Latin verb meaning to run about or to go from one thing to another. Hence, it denotes passing from one topic to another, and is usually marked by analytical reasoning on some subject. The noun "discourse" implies conversation, the verbal interchange of ideas presented usually in an orderly and somewhat extended fashion. In the context of prayer, all discourse arises from love and leads to a more explicit act of love.

A. Three Modes of Praying

While a spontaneous affective dimension exists in all authentic prayer, we can distinguish nonetheless three general modes of praying: saying prayers, meditating and contemplating. The first two of these are discursive, which is distinct from contemplative. In discursive prayer, we are the subjects and the agents of the act of prayer. We *say* (read) prayers: an Ave, a Rosary, the Breviary. We *do* (make) something in prayer: the Way of the Cross, a Novena to Our Sorrowful Mother, the nine First Fridays. We *meditate* on (think about) the mysteries of the life of Christ, our spiritual needs, the Christian virtues. In other words, in all discursive prayer, *we* pray.

In contemplation, on the other hand, God is both the subject and the agent. We remain receptive to his activity within us. God prays us.[1] We *are prayed*.

In a certain sense something of all three modes exists throughout our lives. A little girl learning her prayers for First Communion is taught the Our Father. She says this prayer. She recites it. But, she also tries to think about the meaning of these words to the degree that she is able. Furthermore, this is not merely a formula coming from her or from her teacher. It is especially an expression of her loving communion with God who already abides within her. The other side of the spectrum is also true: A person deeply engaged in contemplation is sometimes moved by God to say or to think about something particular in prayer.

Spontaneous affective prayer spans the entirety of our life. Yet, different modes of praying characterize diverse stages of spiritual genesis. At each stage there is a predominance of one way of praying over others. The saying, reading or recitation of prayers pertain principally to that period of our lives which precedes the critical threshold of immersion. This corresponds roughly to childhood and early adolescence. Meditation, on the other hand, dominates the stage of immersion: our late adolescent and early adult years. The most decisive threshold in our prayer life is the critical threshold of emergence, for there God effects the basic transition from discursive prayer to contemplation. All forms of prayer prior to the inception of contemplation are discursive in nature.

B. Meditation

The term "discursive prayer" refers, therefore, to any form of prayer in which we commune with God through the media of thoughts, images, feelings, gestures, words, signs or symbols. Discursive prayer includes all forms of liturgical and communal prayer; for example: the celebration of the

---

[1]See *Contemplation*, pp. 36-52.

sacraments, charismatic and shared prayer, the chanting of the Divine Office. Such devotional prayers as the Rosary, the Stations of the Cross, litanies and novenas are discursive in nature. Furthermore, certain forms of solitary prayer are discursive, notably meditation.

Meditation is one of the more advanced forms of solitary discursive prayer. Meditation denotes gleaning from a given scriptural passage or a certain mystery of salvation insights and lessons applicable to our day-to-day growth in Christ Jesus. Without excluding other forms of discursive prayer — especially liturgical — meditation is particularly meaningful during the immersion stage of our spiritual genesis.

There exist many methods of meditating: Ignatian, Salesian, etc. There are approaches to solitary discursive prayer which presuppose an already pronounced contemplative bent: the Jesus Prayer, centering prayer, etc. There are innumerable variations, combinations, and emphases which can be grouped under the term "meditation": talking to God about God (adoration, thanksgiving); talking to God about ourselves (petition, contrition); talking to ourselves about God (inspiration, motivation); etc.

Our present treatment of meditation prescinds from all the above particulars — methods, approaches, emphases —in order to glean certain principles common to all. These principles are applicable, *mutatis mutandis*, to all forms of discursive prayer and are most important to both spiritual directors and directees. We group these principles under twelve subheadings. Each of these subdivisions embodies an attitude, a consideration or a concisely formulated principle necessary for discerning the authenticity of the prayer form in question.

(1) TRANSITORY IN NATURE

A first principle concerns the transitory nature of discursive prayer in general and of meditation in particular. The entire stage of immersion is transitory. By its own inner dynamics, it tends to give way to emergence. Consequently, any prayer form particular to the stage of immersion possesses within itself its own principles of self-emancipation and transformation. This truth applies even to the sacraments. Not that we ever outgrow the Eucharist or the Sacrament of Reconciliation as such in this life, but we certainly outgrow our earlier, more discursive, modes of celebrating these sacraments.

At an initial phase of discursiveness we find lots of music, words and movement very meaningful at Mass. The typical parochial liturgy is geared specifically to address this need. However, at a more evolved stage of interior maturity we spontaneously seek to celebrate the Eucharist in a quieter, more low-key and less wordy fashion. Similarly for Reconciliation. "Devotional confession" and detailed examination of conscience were perhaps at one time not only helpful but necessary. We went through pages of general as well as particular examen. But at a more contemplative stage of spiritual development this sacrament accentuates primarily the celebration of our conversion. It is no longer just confession or penance. Even the dimension of reconciliation is transformed into *metanoia* (conversion). At this stage, examination of conscience can be wholly superfluous. The slightest deviation from loving as Christ loves stands out like a sore thumb. There is no way anyone advanced in the spiritual life can possibly hide from his/her actual sinfulness.

(2) MEDIACY

In meditation (as in discursive prayer as a whole), we commune with God mediately; that is, *through some means* such as words, thoughts, gestures, symbols. We repeat ejaculations. We reflect on a scriptural passage. We seek an insight regarding the solution of a specific problem. We make acts of praise and thanksgiving. We pour out our heart and our frustrations to God. In all this prayer, *we* are doing the praying and we are using *some means* with which to communicate with God.

Our activity at this stage is necessary and meaningful. So is the use of concepts, imagery and signs. Nonetheless, meditation is more than what we do or think or feel. It is a response to God's initiative. Even though we are the agents in this prayer, God first moves us. He enables us to pray in every case.

(3) LOVE

Love is the core of all prayer. The purpose of praying is to spend quality time with Father, Son and Spirit. As such, all authentic meditation is grounded in an interpersonal relationship with God, a relationship based upon faith, hope and love.

When speaking of love in the context of prayer, we refer initially to God's love for us (1 Jn 4:10), then to our response in love to him: "We love because he has first loved us" (1 Jn 4:19). When we respond in love to God — or to anyone else, for that matter — sometimes we speak and sometimes we remain silent; sometimes we do something particular ("make love") and sometimes we do nothing (except "just love"); sometimes we hear something, as it were, and sometimes we only listen. In every instance, we receive: We receive our capacity to love so that in loving we are enabled to love more deeply.

(4) FRIENDSHIP WITH GOD

Take the example of two close friends who go apart in order to spend quality time together. They are primarily content to remain in each other's company. Naturally, they will converse some and do certain things, but the crux of their encounter is their *being together*. From this loving presence to one another flow all their interrelating spontaneity and creativity.

They do not worry: What shall I say? What shall I do? How can I avoid lulls in the conversion? How can I manage to fill absolutely every moment with one activity or another? What will I get out of this encounter?

All those questions are absurd when two real friends get together. It would be an insult to prepare a well-ordered speech, even though at times there may be specific issues that they want to discuss. Nor does one monopolize the conversation. Each needs to listen to the other. There is mutual give and take. Listening and speaking alternate, and speaking itself flows out of listening.

Is not God our friend? We are certainly his (Jn 15:14-15). Developing this mutual friendship is the most exigent task of the stage of immersion. Meditation is the key to all quality time spent with God.

Yet, many beginners take a utilitarian, product-oriented approach to meditation. Sometimes outrightly, other times subtly or unconsciously, they look upon meditation as a series of acts which in the end should yield tangible results. When such results are not immediately forthcoming, they conclude that their prayer was a waste of time and effort. They become unduly discouraged and are tempted to abandon meditation altogether.

Unfortunately, some directors reinforce these misguided assumptions with expectations of their own. These directors require that their directees give a detailed account of what happened during every instant of prayer. If the directee is not constantly coming up with consolations or insights, the director probes to discover what is wrong. It goes without saying that directors need to discuss with their directees what transpires during prayer. Yet, this has to be done in an atmosphere which preserves not only the directee's freedom and spontaneity, but God's as well.

There is nothing automatic about meditation. It does not have to yield a predetermined product or result. Meditation is rather a means of enhancing our friendship with God. It evokes a thoughtful and loving response to Father, Son and Spirit dwelling within us. Although meditation employs words and feelings, it is fundamentally a prayer of the heart. Meditation implies an orientation of our whole self to God. Thus, "in meditation we should not look for a 'method' or

'system,' but cultivate an 'attitude,' an 'outlook': faith, openness, attention, reverence, expectation, supplication, trust,
joy. All these finally permeate our being with love in so far
as our living faith tells us we are in the presence of God, that
we live in Christ, that in the Spirit of God we 'see' God our
Father without 'seeing.'"[2]

To the extent, therefore, that images, thought, gestures or
emotions foster openness and receptivity to God, they are to
be encouraged. To the extent that they get in the way, we let
them go. Since spiritual love never requires tangible and
immediate results, this truth can help the beginner realize
that nothing immediately tangible has to happen during
meditation. Frequently, something does occur: an insight, a
feeling of compunction, an inspiration. However, nothing
specifically noticeable has to occur to make the prayer
worthwhile. All true prayer possesses its own intrinsic value,
irrespective of our perceptions.

Those who assume that something particular must always
be going on in meditation often work feverishly to make
something happen. Their meditation becomes an incessant
talking to God, without ever pausing to listen to him. As
soon as a trend of thought ceases, they immediately jump to
another. They try frantically to keep things moving:
thoughts, emotions, whatever. Occasionally, their drive
towards result-oriented activity is such that they turn their
prayer period into a reading session pure and simple.

Others fill up the time for meditation by saying prayers:
the Liturgy of the Hours, the Rosary, the Stations of the
Cross—sometimes all packed within an hour! While these
formal prayers have a place in our lives, they are not meant
to be a substitute for solitary prayer or an escape from the
exigencies of serious meditation.

Sometimes people use time for meditation to plan their
day. They spend this period preparing homilies for others or
thinking over what they have to do next. Naturally, we bring
our whole selves to prayer. But we need to do so without

---

[2]*C. Prayer*, p. 34.

being self-centered. Our frustrations and hurts, our difficulties and concerns are part of our prayer because they are part of our life. However, we frequently let them become also a major source of distraction in discursive prayer. To become unduly introspective about such struggles is not to pray. To become preoccupied with them is to daydream. It is to turn in on self rather than to turn to God.

(5) OUR BASIC STANCE BEFORE GOD

In order to realistically be with God and in him, we have to come to him as we are: with all our individual joys, struggles, thoughts, feelings, moods and concerns. We need not focus directly on these dispositions, unless the Spirit moves us to do so. Rather, we bring our actual selves to God in a stance of faith, hope and love. "Meditation has no point and no reality unless it is firmly rooted in life."[3]

As with an intimate friend, then, we are content to be ourselves without pretense. We are also willing to let God be God. Our fundamental attitude in meditation is this: Here I am, Lord, just as I am — weak, but hopeful; hurting, but being healed; afraid, but with faith in you. In this way we approach meditation in a carefree and open spirit. Content to love God and to be loved by him, we remain praying without undue anxiety concerning what we should be doing, saying, feeling or thinking. In our loving communion with God, we let go all preoccupation with how we *should* pray in order to pray as we *can*.[4]

(6) USE OF A PARTICULAR METHOD

Directees frequently ask: "How should I pray? What method of meditation should I use?" The answers to these questions reside within the directeees themselves, not in

[3]*C. Prayer*, p. 39.
[4]See *Comtemplation*, pp. 72-75 (esp. p. 74).

their directors. Instead of immediately suggesting a particular approach, directors need to help their directees identify the way they desire to pray, their spontaneous inclinations during solitary prayer, the methods they are at home with during prayer. Only in this manner will directees be guided to pray as they can, rather than as someone else thinks they should.

Some find that the Ignatian method of meditation helps them open up to God. Others discover that centering upon a word or verse from Scripture best disposes them to the Spirit. Still others are more at home moving through a rhythm of praise, thanksgiving, contrition and petition during solitary prayer. Whatever the method, it must be approached in a spirit of flexibility and inner freedom. What is meaningful at a given point will surely change, since all discursiveness is transformed in the next critical threshold.

(7) INNER DISCIPLINE

The freedom of spirit which characterizes authentic meditation presupposes inner discipline. It takes a great deal of discipline for freedom, creativity and spontaneity to assert themselves. To listen, to be God-centered, to be responsive to the Spirit are not possible if we are not interiorly mortified. To persevere in actually praying day after day, week after week requires considerable self-discipline and conviction.

(8) NO MAGIC FORMULAS

There are no magic formulas or shortcuts for serious meditation. Most methods or approaches have some value in themselves. Yet, a particular method may or may not be helpful to a given individual, depending upon the manner in which the Spirit is interiorly leading him/her. Any method of meditation is only a means to a goal. No matter how popular a certain method is, it will not be useful for everyone. And what is useful at one point will sooner or later give way to something else.

(9) A FREQUENT DIFFICULTY

An obstacle which some beginners experience in meditation is discouragement and disillusionment on finding that the latest fad does not work for them. Getting nowhere with their efforts and imagining everyone else to be making rapid progress, they agonize: What is wrong with me? Why is it that apparently so many others can pray this way and I cannot? Does God love me less than he loves them? Most of the time, the answer to these questions is simply that God is leading them along a different way. The fact that a certain method of prayer does not work is no indication in itself that one person is less graced than another. Each individual is uniquely graced.

(10) INTERPLAY OF ACTIVITY AND SILENCE

Whatever method of meditation we use, we normally experience an interplay between moments of talking to God and of listening, between moments of reflection and of silence. At the outset of discursive prayer, these silences occur infrequently and for very short periods. However, as we progress, we find ourselves inclined to these silent moments more often and for longer times. While we are drawn interiorly to this increasing silence, the experience of the silence itself can be perplexing: What to do during these moments when activity fades away and nothing appears to be happening?

These silent, listening moments result from a deep contemplative thrust innate to all discursive prayer. Every form of true prayer tends by its very nature towards loving surrender to God. Yet despite that fact, many persons are troubled when they first begin to notice the inclination to remain more quiet. They assume that they should always be doing something in prayer. They interpret these subtle moments as laziness or idleness. They feel guilty for not constantly engaging in some activity.

Spiritual directors do not always recognize the importance of this inclination to remain silent with God. Some directors fail to foster in their directees an awareness of the normality of this tendency. Some ignore it, while others misguidedly advise their directees to make a greater effort to do something during these lulls. They encourage them to work harder not to be silent.

Just as moments of silence are an integral aspect of the encounter between two intimate friends, so silence is an essential dimension of the interchange between God and the soul in discursive prayer. These moments of silence are charged with loving presence. Words are then unnecessary. They would infringe upon the communion. Merton reflects: "It is precisely the function of meditation . . . to bring us to this attitude of awareness and receptivity. It also gives us strength and hope, along with a deep awareness of the value of interior silence in which the mystery of God's love is made clear to us."[5]

On the other hand, spiritual directors encounter persons who have not even seriously begun meditation, but who imagine that they are contemplating. This presumption usually manifests itself in two ways: (a) The silence is self-induced. Some people exert unbelievable effort trying to maintain an emotional and mental blank during prayer. They think that absence of thoughts and feelings equates the *nada* of St. John of the Cross. (b) Others relish so-called prayer which in reality is nothing more than an exercise in fantasizing or nature-gazing. These usually "pray" only when they feel like it. Often, lack of discipline, interior dissipation and laziness characterize not only their solitary prayer but every other aspect of their lives as well.

It is not unusual to find persons just beginning meditation who try to enter precipitously into a form of simplified

---

[5]C. *Prayer*, p. 41.

discursive prayer (e.g., the Jesus Prayer, centering prayer or what is referred to as "contemplations" in the Ignatian exercises). Often, these people need a more active form of meditation. The absence of even a rudimentary self-knowledge and the lack of conscious affection for God in prayer are signs that this is indeed the case.

Directors must steer their directees away from desiring or attempting to fit into some external mold of prayer. There is no substitute for true spontaneity in contradistinction to contrived prayerfulness. Directors must help their directees discover the way of meditation which flows from the Spirit within them. There will be ample time to advance towards more simplified forms of prayer when God is ready.

(11) SUFFERING

Most people in our western societies have very low tolerance for pain. No normal person ever enjoys hurt or directly seeks suffering. Yet, we live in a world which expends so much money and energy on trying to be happy, to have fun, to look youthful. What gives pleasure is judged automatically to be good. What causes pain must therefore be bad. This trend has also infiltrated Christian spirituality. How many people approach prayer expecting to have a "good experience," to attain a blissful feeling, to be bathed with divine consolation! How much energy and time is spent in attempting to procure these things in prayer! As soon as desolation, aridity or some trial presents itself, these persons abandon prayer. Praying is limited only to those occasions when it *feels* good. These persons are like the seed that fell upon rocky soil: "At first they listen to the word and receive it with joy. Yet, they have no roots. They believe for a while, but in time of trial they fall away" (Lk 8:13).

In authentic meditation we alternate between the awareness of being born anew in Christ and of dying to self, of joy and of suffering, of peace and of turmoil. If we are truly receptive to God, we come to realize not only our love for him, but also our infidelity towards him and to one another.

We not only experience God's love, but also our inescapable need for his forgiveness and mercy. Meditation shows us not only our strengths, but especially our limitations and sinfulness. God opens us in prayer to the awareness of our inner poverty. The purifying influence of God's love makes us conscious that we are truly sinners.

If we are to progress in discursive prayer, we must be willing to undergo the suffering integral to spiritual growth: "If you wish to come after me, deny yourself and take up your cross daily and follow me" (Lk 9:23). "Unless the grain of wheat falls to the ground and dies" (Jn 12:24), life cannot break forth from within it.

(12) OPENNESS TO TRUTH

Meditation is not an exercise to insulate us from the truth. This assertion may surprise inexperienced directors who wonder who in the world would ever approach meditation with this attitude. Occasionally, however, we do meet people who try to use meditation to reinforce their egotism or to maintain a certain pious image of themselves. Prayer is not a means for justifying our conformity to established structures or procedures. It is not an escape from risk and change.

On the contrary, authentic meditation disposes us to let the Spirit free us by gradually breaking loose all that fetters us. Thus, meditation gives dying-to-self full vent. It necessarily accentuates our consciousness of our darker side. Merton comments: "All methods of meditation that are, in effect, merely devices for allaying and assuaging the experience of emptiness and dread are ultimately evasions which can do nothing to help us. Indeed, they may confirm us in delusions and harden us against that fundamental awareness of our real condition, against the truth for which our hearts cry out in desperation."[6]

---

[6] *C. Prayer*, p. 103.

We must be willing to accept with equanimity whatever happens in prayer: joy or suffering, consolation or pain, peace or confusion, a sense of the presence of God or a feeling of his absence.

Chapter 7

THE CONTEMPLATIVE ELEMENT OF LIFE DURING THE STAGE OF IMMERSION

There exists a contemplative element in all human life. By "contemplative element" we understand three intimately related entities. First, in relation to God "contemplative" refers to his direct and immediate (i.e., not through any created medium) activity within each person. Second, in relation to ourselves it denotes openness and receptivity to this divine initiative. Third, "contemplative" refers to the abiding, loving interchange between God and each of us: God first loving us and we in turn responding in love.

A. The Contemplative Dimension of Our Life

The very first instant of human existence is an eminently contemplative one. At the threshold of individual creation, God directly and immediately creates a human person. Many laws of nature converge upon that moment, but it is God, out of the superabundance of his love, who produces a unique person. All that we can do at that instant is receive ourselves: receive our individual existence, our personhood, our vocation in life, our call to transforming union in God. Our response in love to his initiative will take a lifetime to express and an eternity to live out.

The very first act of every human being is eminently a contemplative one. The final human act of each person is also eminently contemplative. It constitutes our final "here-I-am," our all-embracive *amen*, our definitive surrender in love to Father, Son and Spirit.[1] Our entire lifetime — all that we have done, all that we have become and all that we have endured — is epitomized in that last contemplative gesture. The sacramental celebration of that moment is Viaticum: "Amen. Come, Lord Jesus" (Rv 22:20).[2]

Our whole earthly sojourn, therefore, exists within two contemplative moments. The contemplative element in our life, then, is that lifelong thread of divine transforming and purifying love operating directly within us and eliciting our faith-filled response in love. We receive this activity, letting God be done in us.[3]

The contemplative element of our life is operative throughout our journey in faith. Normally, the older and more mature we grow, the more conscious we become of its gradually dominating presence. At earlier phases of spiritual development, it was quite operative, even if we did not advert to the fact. At later stages, we benefit from its earlier influences, and in retrospect discover its traces.

A contemplative dimension necessarily exists in all prayer, no matter how formal or discursive that prayer may be. If it is real prayer, there has to be something of the contemplative at its core. We cannot pray unless God first moves us to seek him out. However active our prayer is, there must be some receptivity. Furthermore, prayer without at least the initial stirrings of love is inconceivable.

B. Fostering the Contemplative Element of Life

The awareness of the dominance of the contemplative element in our spiritual life does not occur until we have

[1]See *Contemplation*, pp. 18-20, 32-35.

[2]"Viaticum" comes from two Latin words *via* (way) and *tecum* (with you). Hence the sentiment: May Christ go *with you* on your last *way*, accompanying you on your final passage into eternity.

[3]See *Receptivity*, pp. 133-135.

passed through the threshold of emergence. Indeed, that consciousness and reality are the core of the whole stage of emergence. Yet, already during the stage of immersion there is a gradual awakening to the presence of this contemplative dimension.

Thus, it behooves spiritual directors to encourage this awakening and to foster the development of the contemplative element in the prayer life of their discursively-inclined directees. The following five principles and considerations will help directors discharge this responsibility.

(1) PERSONAL ENCOUNTER WITH GOD

An essential characteristic of the threshold of immersion is a personal encounter with God. We experience Father, Son and Spirit in a mutual, personal friendship. This encounter in turn leads us to seek God within ourselves and within creation by going all the way through everything created.[4]

God wants spiritual directors to capitalize on this personal aspect of their directees' burgeoning relationship with him. Directees need to be brought to a consciousness that the goal of their search is not something, but some-One. It is not enough to consider God as a supreme being, almighty and all-powerful. The personal longings and restlessness of the human heart can never be satisfied by such impersonal attributes. The human spirit pines for personal communion with Father, Son and Spirit.

Moreover, the accent on the personal element in our relationship with God puts the focus where it rightly belongs: on love. Being loved by God, together with loving him and all others in him, is the essence of Christian life.

(2) OUR ACTIVITY

Our activity at this stage conceals a profound contemplative dimension. In their enthusiasm, beginners in the spirit-

[4]See *Receptivity*, pp. 18-23, 114-120.

ual life tend to assume that they are in control of their interior development. Indeed, some even believe that their progress is principally the result of their own doing. The truth of the matter is that our labors to build up a strong self and a better world for Christ are in response to God's initiative and in cooperation with him. Our activity is our contribution to the accomplishment of God's will.

This truth spontaneously tries to impress itself upon the consciousness of those progressing through the stage of immersion. Spiritual directors foster this awareness by helping directees see their activity in proper perspective.

(3) THE USE OF MATTER TO BRING OUT SPIRIT

Our spiritualization occurs in neither an anti-matter nor extra-matter fashion. Instead, it comes about in a way that is trans-matter. We go all the way through matter. In the light of Christogenesis, it is not a question of matter versus spirit or even of matter and spirit, but rather of matter becoming spirit.[5] The word became flesh (Jn 1:14), so that matter can become spiritualized.

By "matter" we understand with Teilhard de Chardin the ensemble of perceptible, tangible reality which constitutes our concrete world.[6] As such, matter reacts with us in two ways. On the one hand, it is a burden. It fetters. it is the prime source of the pain and sin which threaten our lives. "Who will deliver me from this body doomed to death?" (Rm 7:24). Yet, on the other hand and at the same time, matter nourishes us and uplifts us. It attracts, renews, unites. It prods us to growth. Who will give me an immortal body? (1 Co 15:42-53).

Matter is a fundamental principle of both life and death. It is the matrix of our personal transformation and purgation.

At the core of all this matter becoming spirit is the direct

---

[5]See *Receptivity*, pp. 71-72, 115-116, 131-132; *Spiritual Direction*, pp. 27-31.
[6]See *D. Milieu*, pp. 105-111; *Receptivity*, pp. 109-112.

activity of God within our lives. God simultaneously operates immediately within us and through our matter. These two elements together constitute for us the Divine Milieu. God cooperates with the burdening aspect of matter to purge us. He cooperates with the nourishing aspect of matter to make us grow. Both together make up our spiritualization in our concrete world.

Spiritual directors need to help their directees perceive the transforming and purifying activity of God within them in the nitty-gritty of their lives. God works through creatures — our matter — because he is already immediately within us. All mediation on God's part presupposes his direct and immediate presence. This divine initiative pertains to the contemplative element of progress towards spirit.

Furthermore, directors can assist their directees in the area of detachment. Directees must not become fixated on some aspect of matter to the detriment of emerging spirit. The question of detachment pertains to the contemplative dimension of spiritualization, because ultimately it is God who effects our salvific purification. "My Father is the vinedresser." He alone prunes. (Jn 15:1-2).

(4) ASCETICISM

Frequently, beginners in the spiritual life — those in the stage of immersion — engage in self-imposed ascetical practices. Although these neophyte ascetics are basically sincere and are fired with enthusiasm for God, many of their practices are tainted with pride and stem from impatience with God's apparently slow ways, from a desire for control and security, or from imitation of others whom they have read about but have not sufficiently understood.

Directors need to discern carefully with directees their motives for performing ascetical acts. True Christian asceticism always flows from receptivity to God. Self-discipline and mortification are essential to fostering the contemplative element of our lives. A misguided attitude towards asceticism, on the other hand, can prove quite detrimental spiritually, emotionally and psychologically.[7]

The following are some questions which ought to be addressed: Is God indicating that a certain ascetical practice be pursued, or is it primarily the directee's bright idea? Is the directee moderate, balanced and flexible in his/her asceticism? Or, does the directee swing from one extreme to another (like fasting one day and pigging out the next; no smoking one week and three packs a day the next)? Directors need to bring their directees to an awareness that the deepest asceticism of all is that of undergoing God through the daily, faithful discharge of their responsibilities.[8]

(5) SUFFERING

Throughout the stage of immersion, growth and exuberance remain dominant conscious factors in our spiritual development. Suffering and above all death are bad news to the neophyte. We experience ourselves growing in leaps and bounds. We rejoice immensely at our seemingly limitless potential for good.

Nonetheless, in this stage we are already confronted with numerous experiences of suffering: for example, the pain of growing up, the loss of a loved one, being jilted in love, the loss of employment, sudden illnesses, the discovery of certain personal limitations and weaknesses.

Any normal person, therefore, is forced to grapple with the mystery of the cross during the stage of immersion. Our attitude must be one of Christian resignation. On the one hand, we strive with God to resist evil and to alleviate suffering as far as our powers allow. On the other hand, we accept whatever lies beyond our power to change.[9] We undergo this in a spirit of abandonment to God in faith, hope and love.

[7] See *Comtemplation*, pp. 110-115.
[8] See *D. Milieu*, pp. 70-73.
[9] See *Receptivity*, pp. 101-103.

Directors play a major role in helping their directees appreciate God's transforming and purifying activity through suffering. God is primarily encountered beyond our pain. Yet, in a certain sense his presence is also experienced in and through suffering. He cooperates to convert even this to our good.[10]

The ability to suffer in love presupposes an already well-developed sense of the contemplative in our lives. With the cross we receive God, sometimes in spite of ourselves.

[10]See *Receptivity*, pp. 92-101.

THRESHOLD AND STAGE OF EMERGENCE

Chapter 8

EMERGENCE THROUGH CREATION WITH CHRIST

We cannot immerse ourselves indefinitely in creation. Sooner or later we are faced with the inevitable need to emerge through creation with Christ crucified. Thus begins a most crucial threshold in adult spiritual genesis.

Although a certain emergence had already begun in the stage of immersion, what we call the threshold of emergence does not occur until sometime later. This breakthrough marks the point at which we become explicitly conscious of the need to die to self by surrendering in love to Christ Jesus. The soul immersed in creation now desires above all to pass through everything created in order to return with Christ, to the Father, in the Spirit.

Teilhard de Chardin describes this paradoxical interior reversal in this manner: "The joy which we experience in the activity of our lives gives way imperceptibly to a desire to become submissive. The exaltation of growing and producing is gradually changed into a need to die in Another. Having been predominately aware of our attraction for union with God through action, we begin to long for a complementary aspect, an ulterior stage, in our communion with him. Instead of developing ourselves further, we now want to lose ourselves in God."[1]

[1] *D. Milieu*, p. 74.

God's radical intensification of his transforming and purifying love within us, together with an increase in our loving
receptivity towards him, gives rise to this ever more explicit
need to die to self in loving abandonment to him. So radical
is this experience that the very mode of our communion
with God is transformed. We no longer commune with him
principally through images, activities and feelings. From
this threshold on, God himself communes with us immediately and directly in contemplation. At this stage we
become more recipients than agents, more passive than
active, more listening than doing. In this way, a noticeable
contemplative thrust permeates every aspect of our lives.

In the threshold of emergence, we become acutely aware
of the influence of passivities upon us. Indeed, we are
brought to realize this truth as never before: What I call "my
life" is itself far more received in me than it is formed or
"done" by me. My life is not so much mine in the possessive
sense as it is entrusted to me.[2]

Our passivities comprise everything within us, around us,
outside us and in spite of us. They are all that we undergo,
suffer, endure, receive in contradistinction to those things
which we ourselves initiate. From the perspective of the one
to whom they are happening, we distinguish with Teilhard
two forms of passivities: those of growth and those of
diminishment.[3]

Our passivities of growth are those which we experience
as friendly and favorable towards advancement. They sustain our effort and direct us towards what we would consider success. To get in touch with these forces we need to
enter into ourselves in deepest recollection and there ponder
our life at its source. Meditation, reflection and *lectio divina*
in its pristine sense contribute greatly to this salutary
exercise.

Our awareness of the breadth and depth of our passivities
of growth is an important dimension of the stage of immer-

[2]See *Receptivity*, pp. 85-88.
[3]See *D. Milieu*, pp. 76-93; *Receptivity*, pp. 85-103.

sion. Until we have been able to enter profoundly enough into our own being, our immersion in creation necessarily remains superficial.

Yet, the deeper we plunge, the more mysterious we perceive ourselves to be. Entering into ourselves is a frightening experience, and one fraught with risk. It is truly a journey in faith. When pursued to its term this journey can lead only to emergence: not the kind of emergence that is a retreat back up to old familiar surroundings, but rather the emergence which comes out the other side, so to speak. We pass through and beyond ourselves to Christ dwelling within us and in our world.

Appreciation of our passivities of growth leads us necessarily to face head on our passivities of diminishment. These are the forces which we experience as hostile to our progress. They hurt, hamper and thwart what we would normally call success. Yet, in reality these are the passivities most charged with the power to transform us in the likeness of Christ. Although they diminish us exteriorly, they dispose us to grow interiorly.

These passivities of diminishment form the darkest element and the most despairingly useless years of our lives. They consist of our natural failings, physical defects, intellectual or moral weaknesses, illnesses of all sorts, the aging process and death itself.

Unquestionably, our first responsibility is to struggle against these diminishments and actively work with God to reduce to a minimum the evil which threatens us. Yet, however successful this resistance may be, sooner or later we find ourselves vanquished by diminishment. At that point, in order to commune with God we abandon ourselves to him in purified faith, hope and love.

"This is the hour of the specifically Christian operation when Christ, preserving in us all the treasures of our nature, empties us of our egocentrism and takes our heart. This is a most painful hour for our lower nature delivered as it is to the forces which bring diminishment. But it is a salvific hour for the person enlightened by faith who experiences him-

/ herself being liberated from selfishness and dying by the
force of a communion."[4]

A. *The Night of Sense*

What we have been referring to as our passivities of
diminishment, St. John of the Cross calls the dark night of
the soul. The dark night begins for each of us with the
moment of individual creation and it endures till death
inclusive. Yet John does distinguish several stages of the
night. The stage which corresponds with the critical threshold of emergence is the dark night of sense.

The dark night of sense. Each of these words needs some
explaining.

"Dark" is an analogy for painful. Philosophers would call
it "evil." It is what hurts us. It refers to selfishness and
sinfulness. Each of us has a dark or shadowy side. Hebrew
distinguishes dark (*hoshek*) from night (*layil*). As a noun,
hoshek denotes not only darkness, but also calamity and
misery. Thus, it is frequently used to symbolize the pain and
suffering which befall us. "An intense and dreadful darkness
overcame" Abram as God revealed to him the future slavery
and degradation of his descendants in Egypt (Gn 15:12-13).

The dark aspect of the night accentuates all the forms of
adversity which we necessarily undergo throughout our
night. This adversity arises interiorly out of our own inner
poverty: weaknesses, limitations, personal sinfulness. It
assails us also from the outside: a disease, a harsh word, an
unjust accusation. God integrates all this evil into our night,
cooperating with us to convert our endurance of these diminishments into good.

"Night" on the other hand is an analogy for mystery.
True, *layil* sometimes does connote distress and anxiety in
Hebrew. Nonetheless, it is often symbolic of the mysterious
activity of God within us and all around us. It was in the
night that Jacob encountered Yahweh face to face as they

---

[4] *Writings*, p. 261.

wrestled (Gn 32:22-30). It is during the night that the Lord probes our heart and examines us (Ps 17:3). Creation not only proclaims the glory of God during the day, but also "night after night it displays knowledge of him" (Ps 19:2). Even though the Book of Wisdom was originally written in Greek, it still witnesses to the Hebrew symbolism of night: "While gentle silence enveloped all, and night had run half of her swift course, your all-powerful Word leaped down from heaven" (18:14-15).

The New Testament perpetuates the same symbolic usage and distinction: darkness (*skotos*) and night (*nux*). *Skotos* and *skotia* denote moral and spiritual misery. They symbolize the demonic element of our lives. Our evil is "thrown out into exterior darkness" (Mt 8:12). *Nux*, on the other hand, frequently evokes the mysterious workings of God. "It was night" when Jesus entered into his agony (Jn 13:30). God visits us "like a thief in the night" (1 Th 5:2; 2 Pt 3:10). Nicodemus sought out Jesus "by night" (Jn 3:2; 19:39). Usually in the New Testament, the antithesis of light is darkness (rather than night) as in Jn 1:5. But even when night is used in opposition to light, it does not completely lose all nuance of mystery; "There will be no more night ... The Lord God will give them light and they will reign forever" (Rv 22:5).

Thus, the dark night of the soul is truly very painful, but far more importantly it is mysteriously salvific. We reel from the suffering it causes, as we are being filled with the hope which it promises. At first sight we experience far more darkness than night. But in reality there is infinitely more night than darkness. Our darkness is the consuming and purgative side of God's transforming love. All this takes place in mystery.

What then are our senses, in the expression "the dark night of sense"? In the terminology of John of the Cross, these are the senses of the soul rather than of the body.[5] Normally, John does not use the word "soul" in the technical scholastic sense. Rather, he uses "soul" in the traditional

[5]See e.g. *Ascent*, I, 1, 2; *Night*, II, 3; *Contemplation*, pp. 44-52.

mystical sense which derives its meaning from the Hebrew *nephesh* and the New Testament *psyche*. The word "soul" thus denotes the whole human person being acted upon by God, stressing the interior dimensions of our personhood.

St. John of the Cross distinguishes tne senses of the soul from the spiritual part of the soul. That is, he differentiates the more observable aspects of our person from the deepest and most mysterious aspects of the same person. Thus, the dark night of the soul can be viewed basically from two points of view: the night of sense and the night of spirit, the second being a much deeper and more mysterious intensification of the first.

The senses of the human person, therefore, are more than sight, hearing, touch, taste and smell. They comprise also our emotions, imagination, memory, mind and will. Although some of these latter perform spiritual and highly qualitative functions (such as reflection, understanding, loving), they nonetheless pertain to the sensory (or observable) aspect of the soul (or person).

The night of sense is that aspect of the dark night which corresponds to God's loving transformation of us in himself at the threshold and well into the stage of emergence. The immediate cause of the night is transforming union. The principal cause of the darkness (or pain) of the night at this point is our weakness, our resistance, our vacillation, our inner poverty.[6]

B. Signs and Conditions of Authenticity

Is this really the night of sense that I am passing through or am I going off the deep end? Am I truly emerging with Christ or am I digging my own spiritual grave? These questions are very real and very agonizing.

There are basically three signs to look for when trying to discern the authenticity of the night of sense and the threshold of emergence. These signs are also conditions for pro-

[6]See *Receptivity*, pp. 36-41, 48-49.

gress. For, unless they are experienced, a person cannot advance beyond the stage of immersion. The three signs and conditions are: (1) an irresistible drawing towards more quiet in prayer, (2) a mysterious dryness which affects all aspects of our lives, (3) a great deal of anxious concern about what is happening to us.[7]

(1) The first sign in the order of importance, although it is frequently the last one that we notice, consists in a subtle yet irresistible need for more quiet in prayer.

After a lifetime of saying prayers and of much fruitful mental activity during prayer, we discover ourselves wanting to just sit and be quiet with God. We want to listen to him, without necessarily hearing anything at all. We are content to remain silent for a while. Indeed, we need to be quiet. This is in marked contrast to our previous habits of praying.

At first, we are puzzled by the change. The desire for more quiet comes and goes during our periods of solitary prayer. Yet, after some time these urges become more frequent and last longer. We really begin to worry when we discover that we cannot meditate or engage in discursive prayer as before. What is going on within me? Is this loss of prayer — for that is how we tend to interpret the change — due to my infidelity? Am I becoming lazy? Am I losing God?

What is actually happening is quite the reverse. God is beginning to draw us more directly and more immediately to himself. He is progressively leading us into contemplation. Consequently, we are moving further away from our former modes of discursive prayer.

The need for more quiet in prayer gives rise to a desire for longer periods of solitary prayer on a more frequent basis. We are also drawn to seek out not only more interior solitude but more exterior aloneness as well. This is quite a change for a fun-loving, gregarious workaholic.

It is God himself who effects all these changes within us. Moreover, except for a general going-along-with-it-all on our part, he accomplishes these changes without our active

[7]See *Night*, I, 9, 1-9; *Contemplation*, pp. 60-71.

collaboration. These changes are very deep, very intense and all-embracive. They not only affect our prayer as such, but they also influence every facet of our lives: physical, emotional as well as spiritual.

(2) The second sign and condition authenticating the night of sense consists in the profound attitudinal changes which God effects in us as he draws us ever deeper into the mystery of transforming union.

This sign flows from the previous one. As God leads us beyond discursive prayer into contemplation, he becomes more directly operative within our innermost being. This more immediate activity on his part affects our attitudes towards everyone and everything in our lives — God included. The most noticeable change occurs on the emotional level where our gusto and enthusiasm seem to dry up. This aridity is experienced across the board.

No single word can express the paradoxical changes that take place at this time. As we lose interest in nursing or teaching, we become more interested than ever in contributing to the growth of others. As the routine and interactions of conjugal life or religious life become dull and uninviting, we become more committed than ever to the concrete realities of our respective vocations.

Particularly noticeable is the transformation of our value system. Previously, we had been idealistic and uncompromising. Now, we are becoming frighteningly realistic and tolerant of all kinds of weaknesses, even in ourselves. Before, we had been very liberal and active in many respects. Now, we are becoming cautious and content to wait things out. Earlier, we were conservative and opinionated in some respects. Now, we are becoming strangely open, willing to listen and desirous of qualitative change.

What we had thought to be serious sin before — an absolute no-no — is part of our life history now. Moreover, it does not seem all that bad anymore. What we simply could not live without earlier — an absolute must — is now slipping away. Furthermore, we are letting it go gracefully. Our most cherished ideals are tarnished, our dearest expectations are long gone, our most coveted possessions are being drained away. What we would not have dreamt of doing previously, we are now involved in.

Physically, we are slowing down, not just because we no longer have our former stamina, but above all because we strangely want to slow down. Indeed, we have to as a consequence of some indescribable spiritual need. Emotionally, our bubble has burst. We can no longer get worked up over all those things that used to so readily excite us, and we get upset over things that never phased us before. Psychologically, we find ourselves in turmoil and peace at the same time and over the same issues. Spiritually, we have not the faintest idea where we are, where we are going, how we are doing. Previously, we had thought that we were so secure.

All our attitudes are being modified or reversed. We can no longer recognize ourselves. Yet, we sense intuitively that our real self is just beginning to emerge, in spite of us. How on earth can we put all this together?

The cause of this second sign and condition is this: God himself is leading us out of the world of quantity and quantitative appraisal into the more spiritual world of quality. He is drawing our attitudes out of a law and order framework into the realm of purer love and spontaneity. At the threshold of this transformation — which may span years, even decades of our life — we are especially prone to experience confusion, anxiety, even terror at times.

(3) Our concern about all the change taking place within us constitutes the third sign and condition authenticating the night of sense and the passage into the stage of emergence.

Our greatest concern is that we do not know whether we are on our way deeper into God or whether we are falling away from him. We cannot tell whether we are heading towards a breakthrough or a breakdown, spiritually or emotionally. When we try to evaluate what is taking place within us — partly with our cooperation and partly in spite of ourselves — we could just as easily be heading forward or backwards. Most of the surface symptons could be interpreted either way.

The positive sign value in all this lies specifically in the

fact that we are so anxious. A curious sign, to say the least!
Yet it is not so strange when we consider the alternative. If
we were indeed on our way out, we would not care about the
things of spirit. In fact, we would be eager to get out. Our
anxiety to the point of consternation about staying in — in
God's love — constitutes a most crucial sign that this movement is indeed from God and not from us (Rm 7:15-16).

Moreover, the reality of actual sinfulness on our part also
comes into play. If this radical change taking place in us
were not proceeding from God, we would never notice the
discrepancy between Christ living in us (Ga 2:19-20) and sin
living in us (Rm 7:17). Our keen perception of this discrepancy and our painful solicitude in its regard are significant
signs that all this transformation is basically from God.
Consequently, we need to let him take us where he wills.
Faith and trust *in God* (as opposed to faith and trust in
ourselves, in laws or in anything tangible) are integral to this
third sign.

These three signs are hardly what most people would call
consoling, especially when viewed in conjunction with the
three fundamental trials which accompany the night of
sense and the threshold of emergence.

C. Storms and Trials of Sense

Both Christ and sin live simultaneously in us (Ga 2:19-20;
Rm 7:17). However, there is no peaceful coexistence
between the two. As Christ increases within us, he purges us
of the sin to which we cling. In Christ, we thus experience
the depths of our inner poverty.

A basic law of psychology predicates that we facilitate the
release of something deep within us by allowing it to pass
through consciousness. Thus also, we facilitate God's transformation of our deepest inner poverty by allowing ourselves to experience that poverty on a conscious level.

St. John of the Cross refers to the trials that we encounter
in this experience of our poverty as "storms." Temptations

or distractions are terms far too mild to describe the on-
slaught which is unleashed. Storms arise quickly and without
warning. They are sometimes violent and wreak havoc.
While we are in the midst of them, they seem interminable.
They uproot and tear down. They destroy and overthrow so
that something new can spring forth. Storms are an effective
way by which nature prunes and renews itself. Our spiritual
storms come gushing up from within us, and they do not
subside until God has accomplished in us what he has set out
to do through them.

Together with John of the Cross we distinguish three
"storms" which assail the soul during the threshold of emergence and the night of sense. To use John's terminology,
they are (1) the spirit of fornication, (2) the spirit of blasphemy and (3) the spirit of dizziness.[8]

(1) *The spirit of fornication.* This phrase designates the
release of pent-up selfishness of a sexual or lustful order. It
refers also to all our immaturities in the concupiscible
sphere: overeating, excessive drinking, chain-smoking,
addictions of any sort.

During the threshold of emergence most people are especially tempted by the spirit of fornication. God's transforming activity produces in us intense aridity. In reaction, our
emotions search frantically for some relief from all this
dryness. We try to find the greatest pleasure through the
most available channels. For most, that means heightened
eroticism.

(2) *The spirit of blasphemy.* This phrase refers to temptations arising from our irascible appetite: that aspect of the
human person from which emanate anger, impatience,
moodiness, thereby producing a touchy, upset, cranky disposition. Anger can be a healthy human emotion. However,
under certain conditions our irascibility runs wild. Most of
us are not tempted to blaspheme God directly, but if we are
honest with ourselves, we have to admit that we do get angry
and frustrated with him at times.

[8]See *Night,* I, 14, 1-6; *Contemplation,* pp. 85-96.

These times tend to be more frequent and to last for longer periods in the passage of emergence: Why, Lord? Why me? Where are you? What are you doing? Why do you take so long? Will you ever let up? Will you leave me alone? The deep spiritual and psychological upheaval caused by the transformation of immersion into emergence triggers new intensities of irascibility in us. We sometimes reach such a point of anxiety that we do not know whether we can stand any more of God. Yet at the same time, we need him and love him as never before.

This blatant contradiction between blasphemy and tender abandonment confuses us all the more.

(3) *The spirit of dizziness.* In a nutshell, the spirit of dizziness consists in formidable uncertainty, consternation and indecision. We search for answers, but there are none. We find little or no counsel from anyone or anything. Even God seems so far away. Sometimes the reassurance of a spiritual director causes us only more confusion. Finally, we no longer know where to turn. In reality, there are no answers, only surrender to God in dark faith.

No doubt, this is the worst of the three storms. It epitomizes the thrust of the previous two, and it attains the very root of our faith in God. This spirit of dizziness undermines our craving to know exactly what is going on at all times. It shatters our confidence in our ability to be the masters of our own destiny.

The spirit of dizziness is already an introduction into the night of spirit, since God is weaning us of everything short of pure trust and faith in him alone.

These storms are the result of two clashing forces: God directly transforming us and our own inner poverty — specifically, selfishness — resisting his loving activity. Thus, God has to purge us of our egocentrism so that we can be free to respond in love to his initiative. In this sense, God is the cause of our night. But we, together with our innate weaknesses, are the cause of the pain suffered during the night. Our natural limitations are immeasurably compounded by our personal sinfulness as well as by our incorporation in the sin of the world. Furthermore, God's own transcendence and the transforming union which he is so intent upon effecting for us add an increased intensity to our darkness. Teilhard de Chardin expresses this truth especially well: "Being united means in every instance moving on further and dying at least partially in what one loves. But if this being stripped is true in our day-to-day natural lives, how much more thorough must be our detachment when it is a question of giving ourselves to the One greater than ourselves. In this case, therefore, we can set no limits to the uprooting necessary in our journey to God."[9]

The concrete manner in which the above three signs and conditions, together with these three storms, apply to our individual lives is infinitely varied and entirely unique. No two persons ever experience the night in exactly the same way, because no two persons are united to God in transforming love in exactly the same way. Each one of us reflects and experiences God's love in a uniquely individual and wholly personal manner. There are no clones in the spiritual life.

Directors must take all this uniqueness and individuality into account when discerning the presence of these principles in their directees. Each principle will be more or less applicable to each directee at a given point in his/her journey to the Father. Over the long run, however, each of these signs and storms will become apparent in everyone sometime during the stage of emergence, provided of course we live long enough. These are universal principles.

What should spiritual directors advise their directees to do about these signs and storms of the night of sense?

Regarding the signs discussed above, the response is *nada*. We are to do nothing. We must let them happen. These signs are the direct result of God's transforming and purifying activity within us. The Father, and the Father alone, is the vinedresser (Jn 15:1). Anything that we might attempt to do of ourselves in this context would impede God and intensify our weakness. If there is something particular that God wants us to do in the situation, he will make it

[9] *D. Milieu*, p. 88. See *Receptivity*, pp. 48-49, 93-97.

known to us: for example, through a spiritual director, by an inspiration, through common sense and intuition. But unless God indicates something specific, we contribute most effectively to his operation within us by letting it be done.

Regarding the storms: again we are to do *nada*, nothing. Some people react strongly against this advice. We must fight these temptations with every ounce of our strength, they say. We must destroy them before they destroy us. After all, that is what we learned on our mother's knee, in catechism class, in the novitiate.

No doubt something of the above response is applicable in the discursive context of the pre-immersion and immersion stages. But once the threshold of emergence is crossed that approach is rendered inadequate.

First of all, these storms arise not just from us (as an ordinary temptation might), but specifically from God in us: from our innate selfishness coming into direct contact with his transforming activity. God is the principal agent of these storms, and he uses them for his providential purposes: to knock us off our self-made pedestal, to bring us to our knees, to drive us to trust only in him. These are hard lessons. However, in the actual economy of salvation there is no other way to the Father except by way of kenosis: by being emptied (Ph 2:7).[10]

Second, these storms are so much more intense than what one usually understands by temptation. They arise from sources far beyond what our consciousness can possibly penetrate. They originate in our deepest subconscious. When we try to fight these storms directly, one of two things inevitably happens. Either we give in to them out of frustration and fatigue, or we repress them out of desperation. And whatever is repressed eventually comes back even stronger. There is no way that we can win by directly taking on these storms.

What God wants us to do is to undergo them, suffer them, let them run their course. God is cooperating with us in every detail of this ordeal, turning everything to our good.

[10]See *Spiritual Direction*, pp. 20-24.

As we endure these onslaughts, he lures us to be lovingly attentive and to submit to him alone. To fight these storms directly is to rivet our attention on them or on ourselves suffering them, rather than on God.

Let us conclude this chapter by offering some practical advice to spiritual directors.

(1) Directors must have both extensive and intensive understanding of all the above principles (signs, conditions and storms). Furthermore, they need a thorough grasp of the subtle nuances which pertain to these principles. The normal means through which God enables us to attain this competency are serious study, honest self-discipline and prolonged solitary prayer.[11]

(2) Directors have to help their directees realize that the paradox of these signs, together with all the confusion and pain resulting from these storms, is perfectly normal. Moreover, they need to assist directees in seeing that God does not send these things to punish us, but to transform us. He is not an angry judge, but a loving and infinitely compassionate Father (and Mother).[12]

(3) Directees must also be led to appreciate the fact that they will not get through the night unscathed. They will fall occasionally. They will sin. They will inevitably fight God, resist him and say no to him. But God will convert all this to their good, usually even to their greater good. Nothing will effectively thwart his salvific will (Is 55:10-11), nor separate them indefinitely from his love made incarnate in Christ Jesus Our Lord (Rm 8:28-39).

[11]See *Contemplation*, pp. 125-140.
[12]See *Receptivity*, pp. 48-49, 97-101.

Chapter 9

CONTEMPLATIVE PRAYER

At the core of the threshold and stage of emergence is the contemplative orientation of the rest of a person's life. As we have already explained, a contemplative element is operative within our lives from the cradle to the grave. This dynamic attains its definitive breakthrough in the threshold of emergence and becomes increasingly dominant thereafter. In this present chapter, we examine how this critical threshold affects our solitary prayer.

In an earlier book — *Contemplation* — we treated the mystery of contemplative prayer. We do not propose, in this chapter, to repeat that material nor even summarize it (except possibly in a few places, and then only for the sake of clarification). Rather, we present here insights and principles to help spiritual directors guide directees in their experience of contemplation.

By virtue of the universal call to holiness every person is called to contemplative prayer: loving abandonment to God in faith. In rare instances, God gives a particular person a contemplative vocation: that is, a call to a lifestyle which is specifically contemplative. In this chapter, we take up only those principles which apply to everyone called to contemplative prayer regardless of particular vocation. In a forthcoming book we shall treat the principles applicable to the contemplative life as such.

A. Contemplative Prayer and Spiritual Direction

The critical threshold of emergence marks the passage from discursive prayer to contemplation. Perhaps at no other time in our interior journey do we need more the assistance of a knowledgeable, experienced and discerning spiritual director than at this transition. Without proper guidance at this crucial time we can easily obstruct God's transforming and purifying activity within us. Frequently, this obstruction takes the form of forcing ourselves to try to meditate as before, of becoming unduly discouraged by the paradoxes of the night of sense, or of abandoning solitary prayer altogether.

Despite the fact that the Spirit has sparked the subtle, obscure beginnings of contemplation in countless ordinary people, there still remains a dearth of spiritual directors who can competently guide them in contemplative prayer. As far as the ministry of indepth spiritual direction is concerned, we have not improved appreciably since the days of the king-shepherds of Israel. Yahweh laments: "You have not made my weak sheep strong. You have failed to heal the sick and bandage their wounds. You have not brought back the strays or sought out the lost.... For lack of a shepherd they have scattered.... My flock is wandering all over the place and no one bothers to guide them" (Ez 34:4-6).

Directors who follow certain current writers perpetuate the mistaken notion that contemplation transpires only when our mind is blank, only when we experience a tranquil feeling of God's presence, or only when we quiet down and arrive at the still point of our being. These directors place much emphasis on blocking out consciousness of the world around us. Their directees are left with the impression that God turns contemplation on and off, depending on whether we are quiet or in turmoil, peaceful or distracted. These directors imply that the presence of preoccupation, temptation or struggle of itself obstructs God's transforming activity within us and necessarily thwarts our loving response to him.

Authentic contemplation can certainly occur when we feel consoled or when we sense the presence of God. Contemplative prayer can be at work when our mind is empty of all thoughts or images. However, we must never lose sight of the fact that contemplation itself gives rise to intense experiences of night, dread and poverty of spirit. Contemplation can be quite operative when we are being bombarded by tangents, distractions, storms and temptations, provided that we try to keep our loving attentiveness on God in the midst of it all. St. John of the Cross wisely observes: "Neither the sublime communication nor the sensible awareness of God's nearness is a sure testimony of his gracious presence. Nor are dryness and the lack of these a reflection of his absence."[1]

B. Signs and Conditions of Authenticity

Certain signs and conditions authenticate this transition from discursive prayer to contemplation. These signs are universal in the sense that every contemplative soul exhibits them, but each person in a unique manner. These signs are also conditions, because unless they are discernible the transition to contemplative prayer has not yet occurred.

These signs and conditions are basically four:

(1) We experience during solitary prayer an increasing inability to meditate on God or on his mysteries. This inability is relative at the outset of the transition. That is, we can no longer meditate discursively as before, even though we may still be able to meditate some. Gradually, however, this inability becomes permanent.

(2) The inability to meditate can spring from many sources other than God's activity within us. Therefore, a second sign and condition is necessary to back up the first: namely, the disinclination to fix our attention or imagination on anything else either. If we want to daydream, plan schedules or menus, prepare homilies or trips, etc. rather than medi-

---

[1] *Canticle*, 1, 3.

tate, we can be sure that we are not contemplating. We are not praying at all.

This second sign does not preclude the persistence of violent storms and seemingly interminable tangents. These troubling experiences are perfectly normal in authentic contemplation. However, we do not enjoy them, encourage them, or even fight them directly. We remain disinclined towards them, even though we cannot rid ourselves of them. We have to let these tangents run their course, since we cannot effectively stop them. Yet, all the while that we are in prayer we want nothing to do with these preoccupations.

Some of these concerns may be necessary to our vocation in life, as in the case of a professor preparing a class, a mother planning her child's birthday party, a spiritual director trying to attain insight into a directee. All these situations need to be addressed, but not during solitary prayer as such.

The first two signs are expressed negatively: inability, disinclination. The third and fourth signs are positive and give meaning to the previous two.

(3) The third sign consists of an inclination to pray more quietly and more affectively. Although we can no longer meditate on God, we are driven inexorably to place our loving attentiveness in him. The three basic and successive stages of our interior attitude towards God are: (a) God is almighty, savior, provident. This is characteristic of a pre-immersion stage of development. (b) God is friend, companion. This attitude bespeaks the threshold and stage of immersion. (c) God is experienced as Beloved. This dominates throughout emergence, reaching its apex in spiritual marriage. Thus, with the onset of contemplation we not only encounter God in a creature-Creator and friend-to-Friend relationship, but also and specifically as lover to our Beloved. This is the advanced meaning of *agape* (Mk 12:28-34).

(4) The fourth sign is our ability to persevere in contemplation. We persevere in loving our Beloved. Love by its very nature demands consistency and endurance. True love cannot be turned on and off. We cannot fall in and out of

love, if we really love in the first place. Once we love truly, we love forever.

The ability to persevere in wordless, imageless affective prayer for at least an hour a day, week after week, month after month, year after year can come only from God. We may be able to go through the motions for a while. We might be able to fake it for a time. But if our prayer is not authentic, we will inevitably forsake it.

Contemplation is esentially bound with love, and contemplation is at the same time crucifying. Perseverance in contemplation can come only from God who is himself love (1 Jn 4:16) and who gave himself up for each one of us (Jn 13:1).[2]

C. Directing a Contemplative Soul

Many persons perplexed by these changes in their manner of praying seek assistance from spiritual directors. Unfortunately, too many directees find themselves in guidance situations which prove unsatisfactory.

At times, their directors have sufficient theoretical knowledge of contemplation, but lack adequate personal experience. Such directors can sometimes help their directees by pointing out general principles and by giving them an overall view of their progress in prayer. However, these directors are usually quite limited when it comes to helping their directees resolve the myriad of practical problems which occur in contemplation. Moreover, these directors experience great difficulty in discerning the possible authenticity of their directees' solitary prayer, particularly when ambiguities or complications arise.

At other times, directors believe that they have a good grasp of contemplation when in reality their understanding of this mystery is sorely deficient. These directors are ignorant, without knowing it. These can be quite dangerous, because they often proceed from an inflated opinion of their

[2]See *Ascent*, II, 13, 1-9; *Night*, I, 10, 4-6; *Contemplation*, pp. 53-59, 76-84.

own prayer experience together with an inaccurate theology of the spiritual life. For example: Some directors equate true contemplation with centering prayer or with the "contemplations" of the Ignatian exercises. Although both these methods of prayer have a contemplative thrust, they are in fact advanced forms of discursive prayer. Thus, to insist that a directee whom God is calling to contemplation proceed according to principles applicable to these other forms of prayer will frustrate both the directee and God.

At still other times, directors have neither knowledge nor personal experience of contemplation. If such persons are aware of this fact, they must have the honesty and common sense to refer their directees elsewhere. However, some directors who think that there is nothing beyond discursive prayer meddle where they have no business. They wreak havoc. While God is leading directees into contemplation, they try to convince these confused persons that they are no longer praying at all.

Rather than facilitating the directee's response to God, guidance from inexperienced and unknowledgeable directors obstructs or retards progress in prayer. The directee is left suspended on the verge of an interior breakthrough, needlessly fearful of abandoning meditation on the one hand, and unable to allow the Spirit to guide him/her into contemplation, on the other. No wonder St. John of the Cross warns the weary pilgrim: "Watch what you are doing and into whose hands you entrust yourselves, lest you be led backwards.... For, as the master is, so will be the disciple. As the parent is, so will be the son or daughter."[3]

While the inability to meditate as before can arise from the beginning of contemplation, it can also be symptomatic of influences other than the purifying and transforming activity of God within us. Thus, when an incompetent or inexperienced director tries to guide a person who is consistently unable to meditate, one of the following two scenarios usually results.

(1) Although the directee is not positively inclined

[3] *Flame*, 3, 27 and 30.

towards remaining in peaceful, loving attentiveness to God during solitary prayer, the director imprudently concludes that the directee's inability to meditate indicates an immediate call to pray more contemplatively. The director thus encourages the directee to be content with this inability to discourse, while this situation is in reality resulting from a psychological disorder, from pseudo-quietism, laziness, dissipation or from personal sin. Since contemplation has not yet begun in this directee and since s/he has been advised to stop trying to meditate, the directee ends up ceasing to pray altogether.

(2) In an instance in which authentic contemplation is in progress, the inept director insists that the directee continue to meditate as before, despite the inability to discourse and an interior reluctance to do so. This insistence on meditating is often accompanied by nagging probes and questions regarding the directee's moral behavior. The director assumes that the reason for the directee's inability to meditate has to be personal sin. When the directee cannot pinpoint any specific sin as the cause, the director further assumes that the reason must lie in some hidden or past sin. The director continues to badger the directee confusing him/her all the more due to the misplaced emphasis on sinfulness rather than on God's transforming activity. Thus, while the directee is actually making progress, the director is preoccupied with trying to uncover some cause of imagined regression.

Sometimes too, directors tell their directees that by following their inclination to remain quiet they are doing nothing in prayer but wasting time. Pseudo-solutions which such directors impose include the following: (1) They force one new method of meditation after another upon their directees. Of course, none of these methods can prove meaningful or helpful because God is now calling the directee to abandon discursive meditation for contemplation. (2) They encourage directees who regularly spend an hour a day in solitary prayer to shorten the time to fifteen minutes or half an hour. The rationale behind this misguided advice is this:

If directees cannot occupy themselves discursively for one full hour, maybe they can do so for shorter periods. In effect, to follow this advice is to abandon contemplation. (3) Some directors encourage their directees to pray only when they feel like it. They thus make moodiness or caprice the motivating criterion for prayer, rather than faith, conviction and love. (4) Mistakenly concluding that all difficulty with meditation must arise from some emotional or psychological disorder, other directors advise their directees to completely abandon solitary prayer until they discover and resolve their problems. Most people, if they wait that long, will never get started. (5) Still other directors insist on meeting the situation halfway. These counsel their directees to accept their inclination towards interior quiet for brief periods only. After a few moments of "idleness" their directees then have to strive to refocus themselves on some image or word.

All the above pseudo-solutions have this one point in common: They draw persons away from the contemplation to which God is now calling them. A sad situation indeed. "It is as though a portrait of sublime and delicate beauty were daubed with coarse, crude colors by a clumsy hand. . . . And when the work of so delicate a hand as that of Holy Spirit has been roughly treated, who will be able to repair its beauty?"[4]

Such incompetent guidance compounds the anxiety and perplexity which persons normally experience at this time of critical transition. Not only do directees question what they are doing wrong, but also they are forced to doubt the director in whom they have placed such confidence, since directees realize intuitively that the advice is askew. Thus, these persons "believe that they are heading for perdition. Moreover, their directors encourage them in this belief and parch their spirits by taking from them the precious gifts which God is bestowing on them in solitude and silence. . . . Their directors plunge them into mire and mourning. These

[4] *Flame*, 3, 42.

souls are losing one thing and laboring without profit at another."[5]

Directors who do not understand the way of spirit should refrain altogether from attempting to guide a contemplative soul. They should have the honesty and humility to refer the directee to a competent spiritual director. If no such director is available, it is better to have none at all. God will furnish the soul with guidance through some other means: a homily, study, a chance encounter, interior inspiration, etc.[6]

Spiritual directors must approach each directee in the only manner that God intends: "Let them always remember that the principal agent, guide and mover of these souls is not the director, but the Holy Spirit. They themselves are but his instruments."[7]

Spiritual directors have to maintain a stance of openness and receptivity to God as he operates within each directee. Directors need to wait for God to reveal himself in his time and in his way. Directors must let the initiative rest with God, and refrain from any attempt to control, manipulate or dominate directees or God's activity in them.

Essentially, the role of spiritual directors with respect to the contemplative soul is to prepare the way for the Lord (Mk 1:3), letting God himself direct the soul by ways and means that neither the soul nor they can possibly understand. Directors are only weak "instruments to guide souls in the way of perfection by faith and the law of God, according to the spirit that God is giving to each one. Let them, therefore, be careful not to guide these souls according to their own way or in a manner suitable to themselves."[8]

Solitude, silence and freedom of spirit form the most normal milieu in which we open ourselves to the immediate and direct activity of God within us. In this atmosphere God surrenders himself to us in love, imparting a peaceful and loving communion with himself. Initially, we do not per-

[5] *Flame*, 3, 53.
[6] See *Spiritual Direction*, pp. 51-53.
[7] *Flame*, 3, 46. See *Spiritual Direction*, pp. 83-94.
[8] *Flame*, 3, 46.

ceive this truth. We are too aware of all the darkness, aridity and emptiness. Yet God is present and the grace of contemplation is hard at work. Frequently, the last person to realize that contemplation is truly operative is the very person who is experiencing it. For contemplation infinitely transcends our perceptible and tangible world. In time, however, we slowly become aware that welling up from beyond the darkness, aridity and emptiness is a delicate, subtle, ineffable joy and peace.

To help directees enter into solitude of heart and freedom of spirit, spiritual directors should allow sufficient liberty with regard to discursive prayer. Earlier in the directees' lives directors may have suggested material for meditation. Now, they need to encourage their directees to choose what they are drawn to. Previously, directors had encouraged perseverance at discursive prayer. Now, they have to advise the same directees to let go meditation. At this time God is secretly imparting to these directees his own wisdom. Therefore, any effort on their part at this time to meditate or become involved discursively disturbs their interior recollection and obstructs God's transforming and purifying love.

Thus, "if they try to work on their own in this context or to do anything other than remain quiet and receptive in that passive and loving attentiveness [which is contemplation] they will impede the blessing which God is communicating to them."[9]

When there is positive indication that God is leading directees into contemplation, the director must encourage them to let go all effort, concern and even desire to pray discursively. S/he must counsel them to be content to remain in a peaceful, loving attentiveness towards God. The director needs to support them in this direction, even though they may think that they are wasting their time and could be doing something more profitable.[10]

When God calls us to contemplation, our imagination,

[9] *Flame*, 3, 34.
[10] See *Night*, I, 10, 5.

memory, emotions and mind should not be bound to any particular object. We may be moved to use a scriptural word or an image as a means to interior recollection. However, in relation to contemplation as such, this word or image serves merely as a springboard — a disposing factor — to that wordless, imageless communion with the indwelling Trinity. Moreover, in the course of contemplation, should we be moved to something tangible — a feeling of compunction, an act of thanksgiving, a petition, the repetition of a phrase, etc., — we are to follow the prompting as far as it leads. Once it has passed, however, we should interpret its going as God's sign that he again wants us to return to imageless and wordless loving communion with him.

Chapter 10

THE SACRAMENT OF EMERGENCE

In God's plan of salvation, he has given us certain sacraments to celebrate the more decisive moments of life. The sacraments, therefore, play a significant role in personalizing many of the critical thresholds of our spiritual journey.

Baptism celebrates our individual creation and formally incorporates us into the mystical Body of Christ at the earliest possible age. Confirmation ratifies the Christian commitment begun in Baptism and celebrates our immersion into God's world for Christ: our active and voluntary participation in the building up of his Body. Our passage from this world into eternity — our personal death — is sacramentalized by Viaticum: a special Eucharistic celebration launching us on our "way" to consummate, transforming union in God.

What then is the sacrament of the threshold of emergence? It is the Eucharist.

A. The Eucharist

In its most general sense, a sacrament is a visible, tangible sign of an interior, mysterious reality. A sacrament not only says something of our interior life, but also it effects something within us. A sacrament is a special incarnation of God in our world, both individual and collective. Hence, the person and mission of the Word made flesh is the sacrament of God's abiding love and mercy towards each one of us and towards all of us. The Church as the corporate body of believers in Christ extended into space and time is the sacrament of the spiritual dimensions of Jesus's life and ministry. The Eucharist is the sacrament par excellence of the Church's sacraments, since it is the sacrament of the Body and Blood of the Lord in his paschal mystery (i.e. in his death and resurrection) extended into every place, for all time.

The Eucharist comprises several basic aspects: the Mass, the reservation of the Blessed Sacrament in a church or oratory and Communion whether taken to the sick or as Viaticum. From the dawning of the use of reason to death, the Eucharist is the spiritual nourishment of each pilgrim on life's interior journey.

The Eucharist as Mass is the sacrament par excellence of the contemplative. And since the threshold of emergence marks the definitive contemplative breakthrough in our life, the Mass has a most special rapport with every facet of the stage of emergence.

Particularly since Vatican II, there has been a concerted effort to adapt the liturgical setting of the Mass to specific needs and cultures. The guitar and castanet Mass of a Mexican mission is very different from the pipe organ and choral celebration in a St. Patrick's Cathedral. There are the special Masses for children, specified Eucharistic liturgies for the communal celebration of Reconciliation and the Anointing of the Sick, etc. The usual parish Masses are geared to appeal to persons approaching or moving through the stage of immersion. As the contemplative element in our life matures during the stage of emergence, we spontaneously seek a more low-key, quietly prayerful liturgical milieu for our Eucharist celebrations.

This sort of adaptation can be expressed in as many ways as there are contemplatively inclined communities and celebrants. In this chapter, however, we do not address that myriad of variations. Rather, we discuss the specific dimension of the Mass which embodies sacramentally the deepest yearnings of the contemplative soul, regardless, of liturgical setting.

There are many theological dimensions to the Mass: communal, sacrificial, worshipful, etc. The dimension which is most directly in tune with the contemplative spirit is the Eucharist as mystery.

During every celebration of the Mass three aspects especially epitomize the mystery-contemplative dimension of the Eucharist. These are: the passover of the Lord, the "do this in remembrance of me," and the "mystery of faith." Needless to say, every part of the Mass can be of special significance to the contemplative soul: the liturgy of readings, the homily, the offertory, etc. The three that we single out, however, when understood in their full context, comprise the gist of all the others.

B. The Passover of the Lord

The full passover of the Lord extends from the beginning of time to the parousia (i.e. to his final and definitive coming: Mt 24:3). "He is the firstborn of all creation. In him were created all things in heaven and on earth: visible and invisible. . . . All creation is held together by him . . . and he reconciles everything in himself" (Col 1:15-20). Through the person of the Word everything that has been, is now or will be comes into being (Jn 1:3). Furthermore, towards the person of the resurrected Christ all creation is converging as towards an Omega point. Everything is through him, with him and for him. All this witnesses eminently to the contemplative dimension of creation.

This mystery which comprises the totality of created existence is uniquely sacramentalized in the twofold consecration of the Mass: "This is my Body. . . . This is my Blood."

Two of the most contemplative aspects of the mystery of Christ are epitomized in the simple gesture of the consecration of the bread and of the wine. In virtue of the first consecration, Christ comes. He comes forth from the Father to this specific place at this moment in time. In virtue of the second consecration, Christ goes. He returns symbolically to the Father in perfect love and total submission to his will.

The symbolism of this coming and going is couched in the Semitic anthropology of living and dying. Although at the Last Supper Jesus admittedly spoke in Aramaic (a dialect related to Hebrew), he nevertheless used the Hebrew mentality as a basis of his Eucharistic words. To the Jews of his time the living human person was an integrated whole. But this person could be seen from several points of view. There is the perspective of *basar*, that of the exterior, corporeal person: the body. There is the different perspective of *nephesh*, that of the interior, spiritual person: the soul. And there is the further perspective of the *hayyim*, that of the living or life-filled person.[1] Now, *hayyim* resides in the blood. What happens in death? The life residing in our blood is separated from our *basar* (body) and *nephesh* (soul), both of these latter going into the grave.

At the consecration of the bread Jesus, applying the language of sacrifice to himself, transforms the substance of the bread into himself: "This is my body" (my *basar*, and by implication my *nephesh*). This is I, he says in effect. Christ comes forth in mystery from the Father and is sacramentally rendered present in a particular place and time under the appearances of bread.

Yet, that represents only part of his mission. By his love and obedience unto death, death on a cross (Ph 2:8), Jesus thereby returned to the Father completely transformed. This truth is sacramentally re-presented in the separate consecration of the wine: "This is my blood."

Historically, Jesus himself separated these two consecrations at the Last Supper by the paschal meal (Lk 22:19-20). Thus, when Jesus separates his Blood (in which resides his *hayyim*) from his *basar* (and *nephesh*), he symbolizes in mystery his physical death on the cross, together with his

---

[1]There are also other perspectives: *lebh* (that of feelings, sensitivity, heart), *ruah* (that of breath, spirit), etc.

resurrection and ascension. Jesus died in order to rise glorified and thus return transformed to the Father.

This symbolism may at first appear foreign to Western mentalities. However, a more prayerful reflection on these concepts and terms reveals a very simple, but powerful truth: The once and for all passover of the Lord is actually, though sacramentally, re-enacted for each of us at this time and in this place.

Christ's passover is multiform. It comprises the totality of creation which is through him, in him and for him. It comprises in a most concrete way his incarnation, death and resurrection. It is re-presented sacramentally in the twofold consecration of each Mass until the end of time.

Transformation, love, submission, receptivity, coming forth, return — all this bespeaks eminently the contemplative element in each person.

C. Do This in Remembrance of Me

"Do this in remembrance (or as a memorial) of me" (Lk 22:19; 1 Cor 11:24-25). These words contain a world of meaning. The Hebrew verb which underlies the Greek expressions of Luke and Paul is *zakar*. It is translated: to remember, to recall, to record, to make a memorial offering. The noun *zeker* signifies, therefore: remembrance, memorial, recollection, memory.

We should not, however, confound *zeker* with our Western mode of thinking of monuments. The Lincoln Memorial in Washington, D.C. is an inspiring tribute to the sixteenth president of the United States, but it does not come close to the depth of meaning expressed by *zeker*. One cannot but be deeply moved standing in front of the book depository building in Dallas and looking up at the top floor, corner window whence came the shots that assassinated John F. Kennedy. One can see those events actually recorded on film and remember the pain of the nation in mourning. But as vivid as those memories may be, they cannot begin to compare with *zakar*.

When we remember, we go back into the past. *Zakar*, on the other hand, transports the past into the present. It re-presents a previous event, not just represents it. In the case of the Eucharist, the paschal event of Jesus is symbolically re-enacted here and now in mystery.

It comes about this way: Christ charismatically present in the presbyteral charism of the celebrant, renders the Christ-event actually, though sacramentally, present. In the Eucharist we do not merely "recall" Jesus' death and resurrection. Rather, we become real partakers in that event which is celebrated sacramentally and in mystery.

Thus, the Eucharist is infinitely more than "the Liturgy." Granted, the Mass does take place within a particular liturgical setting. However, the Eucharist itself far transcends the context in which it is expressed.

Moreover, the celebrant does not "say" Mass. He celebrates it. Furthermore, he receives it, since Christ himself celebrates his own Eucharist through the priest. When we hear, "This is my Body," it is Christ speaking and transforming. It is really *his basar*. It is he himself.

The transformation of the bread into Christ is symbolic of our personal transformation into his likeness (2 Cor 3:18). The transformation of the wine into Christ is symbolic of our dying and rising with him. This transformation is eminently contemplative, because God himself is effecting it in a mutual exchange of love.

D. *The Mystery of Faith*

The introductory phrase of the Mass's memorial acclamation is "Let us proclaim the mystery of faith." Each of the various responses which follow expresses in its own way the passover of the Lord together with its *zeker*. That introductory phrase adapts an exhortation from Paul to deacons: "Hold on to the mystery of faith with a clear conscience" (1 Tm 3:9). It embodies also a very rich Hebrew attitude: *aman* (from which comes the word *amen*).[2]

---

[2]See *Contemplation*, p. 33.

The basic meaning of the verb *aman* is to stay or to support. It can also signify to nurse an infant or to rear a child. Intransitively, it means to be firm, to be true, to be faithful. Hence, in a deeper sense, *aman* is to trust, to confide in, to believe in. *Emet*, a noun derived from *aman*, indicates an essential quality of God: firmness, stability, faithfulness, fidelity. *Emet* is frequently associated with Yahweh's *hesed*: his tender loving care for his people.

Therefore, we proclaim not only "the mystery of faith," but also the mystery of fidelity: of God's incomprehensible faithfulness to each one of us. What is our response to this inexorable mystery? Faith. Faith in Christ Jesus. Moreover, this faith translates itself concretely in an interior attitude of loving receptivity, of faithful obedience to God.[3]

This attitude of loving receptivity reaches its Eucharistic climax in our personal reception of communion. At the consecration of the Mass, Christ renders himself present upon our altar. At communion, he comes to us so that we can individually and communally return with him to the Father: his Father and ours.

The act of communing is the gesture par excellence of comtemplative prayer. It is the sacrament of God's loving, abiding, transforming and purifying activity within us. Communion is the sacrament of the Trinity's communion with each of us and of our union with one another in Christ.

[3] *See Spiritual Direction*, pp. 175-177.

THRESHOLD AND STAGE OF PERSONAL CONVERSION

Chapter 11

PERSONAL CONVERSION

The breakthrough which we discuss in this chapter is unique among the six critical thresholds of adult spiritual genesis. It is unique for several reasons: (1) Post factum, a person can frequently pinpoint the very day, hour and minute when it occurred. (2) Normally, this particular conversion experience happens only once in a lifetime. (3) Although most often it epitomizes the stage of emergence and serves as an introduction into the night of spirit, personal conversion can take place at an earlier stage in life.

The relationship of personal conversion to emergence is important. Even when in a given instance the conversion experience itself occurs at an earlier time, its full effect is not realized until near the completion of the stage of emergence. Personal conversion is to emergence what Confirmation is to Baptism. It is like the second step or the other side of the coin. The threshold and the stage of emergence frequently extend over many years, even decades, of a person's life. Personal conversion, on the other hand, usually takes place in the blink of an eye. In an instant it epitomizes all the factors which have been converging since individual creation.

A. Conversion

The word "conversion" very aptly conveys the interior reality which this threshold designates.

The Hebrew scriptures are replete with insight into the

mystery of conversion. The ancient Israelites did not find it necessary to invent a special term to express their view of repentance. They chose a very common word — *shuv*, to return — and gave it a theological meaning.

Historically, the Hebrews at first developed cultic and external forms of repentance. Chief among these penitential observances was fasting to which wailing, sackcloth and ashes were added. All this was supposed to appease the wrath of God for transgressions of the Law.

Several of the great prophets sharply criticized the superficial and legalistic attitude which permeated many of these penances. Isaiah, Amos, Hosea, Joel, Zechariah are among the most outspoken. "Rend your heart, not your garments" (Jl 2:13) is their typical response to these ritualistic practices. The psalmist minces no words: "Sacrifice gives you no pleasure, Lord. Were I to offer you a holocaust, you would not accept it. My offering, O God, is an open and contrite heart. This you will not spurn" (Ps 51:16-17). This criticism is not an all out repudiation of penitential liturgies as such, but an attempt to situate them in their proper context. Joel expresses the proper balance: "Turn to me your God with all your heart, and then with fasting, weeping and mourning" (2:12).

Thus, the prophets imbue *shuv* with the basic notions of turning towards and returning to God. Yahweh himself is the focal point of this movement. We must turn to him in obedience to his will and with complete trust in his love. But concretely, we are sinners. Therefore, our turning is also a returning, since we have in effect strayed from him.

The New Testament picks up these insights and gives them their greatest possible fullness in the person of Jesus. The primitive Christian community chose a rarely used Greek word and endowed it with a theocentric meaning: *metanoeo*, to repent; *metanoia*, conversion (and on occasion *strepho*, to be changed). Literally, the verb means to undergo a change of mind and heart, hence to convert (Lk 17:3-4). It means also to experience a change of principle and practice, hence to reform (Mk 1:4).

The keynote of the preaching of John the Baptizer — the

last of the great prophets of Israel — is *metanoeite*: be converted (Mt 3:2). This slogan of John is familiar to his Jewish contemporaries, but he gives it a wholly new significance. Conversion is once and for all. It must be from within and not in appearance only. Conversion is demanded of everyone: notorious sinners (Lk 3:12), Gentiles (Lk 3:14) as well as righteous Jews who do not think they need it (Mt 3:7-10). This interior change must be translated into a corresponding life of love and obedience to God's will (Lk 3:10-14) . John celebrated these conversions with a sacramental act of transforming purification: a baptism of *metanoia* (Mk 1:4; Mt 3:11). Through this baptism God fashioned for himself a community of converted ones who were given special responsibilities in the ultimate conversion of humankind. Hence, *metanoia* is both God's gift and our task.

According to Matthew and Mark, *metanoeite* is literally the first word spoken by Jesus in his public ministry: Be converted. Believe in the Gospel. The kingdom of God is within you (Mt 4:17; Mk 1:15). Jesus makes conversion the fundamental requirement for faith in him. The very purpose of his mission is to call us to *metanoia* (Lk 5:32). The Father's revelation in Christ demands unswerving decision on our part. It requires a radical conversion, a resolute turning to God in unconditional obedience, and consequently a turning from sin (Mt 4:17; 18:3).

Conversion in this sense is irrevocable. There can be no turning back once God has turned our entire being towards himself. *Metanoia* is holistic. First and foremost, it attains the inner core of our being. But it also affects all our attitudes and conduct. Jesus's call to conversion is addressed to everyone without distinction. It is the only way to salvation.

The commitment of conversion and the commitment of faith in Christ Jesus are one and the same. Neither are accomplished by our initiative or achievement. God brings them forth from within us. Jesus shows from the example of a child what "to be converted" means to him: to be little, to know one's need, to be receptive before one's loving Father

(Mt 18:3). The effects of personal *metanoia* are: being poor in spirit, mourning and repenting for one's sins, being meek and humble of heart, yearning for God in himself, striving for peace and laboring for true progress, wholeness of being, selflessness to the point of suffering persecution for all that pertains to God and his world (Mt 5:3-10).

For all its pain and uprooting, being converted does not drive us to the torture of penitential works or to despair. Rather, it awakens us to joyous abandonment to God. *Metanoia* is no longer law as in Judaism, but Gospel pure and simple.[1] It is "good news" beyond our wildest imagination.

B. Personal Conversion

"Conversion" is surely the best word to describe the threshold which we are discussing. Nonetheless, the word does need to be modified. Conversion as such is an ongoing process. Yet in this context, we are treating specifically of one moment in that lifelong development.

Quite literally, conversion begins with individual creation. In that instant when we come into being, God has already turned us to himself. That truth is at the core of the universal call to holiness. This turning to God is what gives meaning to our personal vocation, not only at our inception but throughout life. There is even a sense in which this initial turning to God is the start of a returning to our Father, with his Son, in their Spirit.[2]

Moreover, our lifelong process of conversion can never reach its ultimate and definitive threshold until death. Death is *the* decisive threshold of our turning to God, of our change in God (transformation), of our return to the Father — in a word, of our deification.

Yet, there are normally several significant breakthroughs

---

[1]See G. Kittel, ed., *Theological Dictionary of the New Testament*, IV, Eerdmans, 1967, pp. 975-1008.

[2]See *Spiritual Direction*, pp. 20-23.

in our conversion process. One of these is pivotal. It epitomizes all the converging elements which precede it, and it launches us into a radically new intensity and consciousness for the rest of our spiritualization.

The question still remains: What term do we use to describe this pivotal instant in our ongoing conversion?

Moralists sometimes employ the phrase "fundamental option." There is truly an option involved in the turning point which we are considering, and God knows, it is fundamental. However, fundamental option in the moral sense is also rightly said of other peak experiences in life. To apply "fundamental option" only to this instant of conversion would be to unduly restrict the reality underlying that phrase.

Classical spiritual authors frequently refer to this moment of *metanoia* as "second conversion." The adjective "second" is used in contradistinction to "first conversion" which in their theological framework is Baptism (ordinarily in infancy). There is something to be said for this phraseology. Yet it has at least one obvious drawback: namely, what they call "second conversion" may in actual fact be our third, fourth, or fifth threshold of conversion. First Communion may have been our second, Confirmation our third, matrimony or religious profession our fourth, and so on.

Others prefer to qualify this unique moment in the whole conversion process with adjectives such as: basic, radical, etc. Up to this point, we have used the term "pivotal." This unique instant is all of these and more. Therein lies the problem of finding the appropriate combination of words. This threshold comprises so much in its simplicity and has such far-reaching effects in its power that it defies our ordinary modes of expression. It is like trying to *imagine* the pure listening of contemplation (i.e. just listening to God without expecting to hear anything at all).[3]

We have settled on the modifier "personal": personal conversion. Even this term has its limitations, but it has also

[3]See *Contemplation*, pp. 36-43, 146-147; *Spiritual Direction*, pp. 61-66.

some very obvious strengths. This moment in our conversion process is particularly personal. Every facet of our personhood converges upon that instant and our whole life up to that point is epitomized in the utter simplicity of the decision which is made. So much so, that the only other instants in life which can be compared with the intensity of this moment are spiritual marriage and personal death.

In our personal conversion, all that is deepest and most characteristic of our unique personhood comes to the fore as never before: consciousness, decision, commitment, love. Once they have come forth, they then remain in the forefront for the rest of our earthly sojourn. This is the highpoint of our interior life, our peak spiritual experience of them all, thus far. This moment is fundamental, basic, radical, pivotal in relation to all others.

What are some of the more salient characteristics and paradoxes of personal conversion?

Usually, the actual threshold of this experience and all its major effects occur and are made manifest at the same time. For most people this threshold marks the point of synthesis for all the converging elements which comprise the stage of emergence. But occasionally, for God's own mysterious reasons, the threshold of personal conversion occurs earlier in life. In that case, the full effects of that conversion experience do not become apparent until the stage of emergence is nearing completion. In this instance, one's personal conversion may seem to transpire over a long period of time. Whether it happens all at once or is protracted over years makes no real difference. It will happen in God's way and at his time for each of us.

The most important characteristic of our personal conversion is that God directly effects it. The fundamental option, the radical decision and the unconditional commitment which are part and parcel of this conversion experience constitute our personal response to his initiative. We convert because we are converted. We turn because God turns us irrevocably to himself. We change because we are changed. Yes, it is *my* conversion, but in the sense that "I live now, no longer I, but Christ lives in me" (Ga 2:20).

Our cooperation at this moment is paramount. This act of conversion is eminently an act of our whole person: all our feelings, attitudes, weaknesses and strengths. All are synthesized, refined, purified and transformed by God in that instant. It is the moment par excellence when our maximum of effort and action coincides with our optimum of receptivity to God.

For all the power and intensity of our personal conversion, we still remain sinners until death. Moreover, we are still capable of serious sin. Indeed, all sin at this stage in life is serious to the conscientious pilgrim. Twenty and thirty years after his conversion Paul is still acknowledging his personal sinfulness: "I am fleshy" (Rm 7:14-25). "I am content in weakness" (2 Co 12:7-10). "I have not yet been perfected" (Ph 3:12-16). The thrust of our commitment in faith and love to God may be unconditional, but we are still very weak and in need of much transforming purification. Our option and decision may be basically irrevocable, but we are not yet whole. Far from it! We still have the night of spirit to go through, plus many years of searching, healing, yearning and struggling.

Interiorly, the moment of personal conversion is traumatic, in some instances second only to death itself. But exteriorly, the concrete surface circumstances which surround this threshold can be utterly common and banal. It can take place while jogging, at a party, during a wake. A person may be strolling in the woods, driving a car, relaxing in an easy chair. One was resting under a fig tree (Jn 1:48-49). Another was on a journey (Ac 9:1-19).

Whenever and however it occurs, the soul experiencing its personal conversion always hits rock bottom. What constitutes rock bottom for one person can be vastly different for another. Nonetheless, for each of us this pivotal conversion cannot take place until we have been reduced by God to a clear-cut, either-or choice: God or self. No frills, no if's, no maybe's, no but's: One or the other. At this stage of interior development, we can freely choose only God. Yet the wrenching effect of letting go self is beyond description, and it will be played out concretely for the rest of our mortal life.

In that instant of personal conversion we reach a perfectly simple existential inability to do other than to fling ourselves wholesale into God.

This moment in our life is so radical because, short of spiritual marriage and death, it is the closest we get to the pure "now" of eternity. Time seems to stand still for that instant of stark encounter with God. Then, of course, time starts up again and we have the rest of our life to live out this personal conversion and to let it be translated into every fiber of our being.

In personal conversion we come face-to-face with the living God (Gn 32:31). We encounter the resurrected Christ person-to-person beyond all sensory perceptions: uncreated divinity in direct contact with our created individualities. We can never be the same from this moment forward, nor do we want to be.

Thus, this intensely spiritual *metanoia* experience needs embodiment. On a day-to-day level, our ministry and vocational lifestyle are directly affected. Our sense of mystery, conviction, God-centeredness is immediately sharpened and intensified. Interiorly, our life is also deepened immeasurably. Our faith in Christ Jesus is more conscious and unswerving. Our hope in God becomes a yearning, a "straining forward for what is yet to come" (Ph 3:13). Our love of God is transformed into passionate surrender to our Beloved. These embodiments take on a thousand and one shapes and forms week after week, month after month, year after year.

Three final notes regarding personal conversion need attention.

(1) Because of the degree of consciousness and decision which accompany the crossing of this threshold, many people can pinpoint the very time and place that their personal conversion occurred. In other cases, however, God ekes out personal conversion so subtly that some individuals cannot even be sure what year it took place. Yet they still know without any hesitation that it has in fact happened. Therefore, if a person does not know whether or not his/her

personal conversion has occurred, s/he can be sure that it has not.

(2) The second note is this: Personal conversion in some lives is accompanied by an unexpected change of commitment. Our commitment towards God is, or course, intensified as never before. That change is expected. What we are referring to here, however, is the unexpected change of commitment on the part of some people towards what is commonly called "vocation," "ministry" and "lifestyle." In some cases, a teaching sister receives a contemplative vocation, a monk becomes a hermit, a truck driver seeks the permanent diaconate, an unassuming mother of five opens a halfway house for derelicts. However, one's change of commitment can go the other way too — a way which might shock some "pious souls." A spouse may finally have the courage to seek an annulment for a failed marriage in order to remarry. A sister may have to leave her religious community in order to pursue God at the depth he is now demanding. A priest may have to seek a dispensation from ecclesiastical celibacy in order to be true to himself and to God's mysterious movement within him.

(3) The third note is this: An unanticipated and unsought gift sometimes emerges from personal conversion. We are referring to the charism of being a spiritual director to others: becoming an *abba* or *amma*.[4]

Some persons, having experienced their personal conversion, need spiritual direction as never before. Others are henceforth called to minister spiritual direction as never before. In either case, God remains the only director of souls, and he continues to use us as he wills.

Yet, even those not called to be spiritual directors in the traditional sense are nonetheless called to be spiritual leaders and animators in their respective families, communities and parishes. Our personal conversion has a centrifugal force about it. Love by its very nature tends to spread itself around.

[4]See *Spiritual Direction*, pp. 33-50.

Chapter 12

EXPERIENCES OF PERSONAL CONVERSION

Our discussion of personal conversion would not be complete without some actual accounts of this experience. The following three examples are chosen for two principal reasons: (1) Each person is relatively well known. Therefore, the broad lines of his/her growth in Christ are common knowledge. (2) Each of these saints describes his/her own personal conversion in an autobiography. Therefore, we are presented with a direct witness to the event rather than second or thirdhand interpretations.

We encourage the reader to go directly to the sources in order to see the simplicity and power of the respective conversion experiences in their original contexts. In the following presentation of these three accounts, we adhere as closely as possible to the author's own words. We do, however, make observations and summations as the situations warrant. In view of the previous chapter, any further theological reflection on the commonalities of these three personal conversions is kept to a minimum.

A. St. Augustine of Hippo (354-430)

Augustine describes his personal conversion in the *Confessions* (bk. 8, pars. 1-30). He was thirty-two years old and had been uncommonly bright and resourceful all his life. He pretty well got whatever he wanted and excelled at whatever he put his mind to. For some time already his soul had been half- Christian and half-pagan. In a sense he relished having the best of both worlds. Yet, in a deeper sense he anguished at not being able to resolve the dilemma. He immensely enjoyed *la dolce vita*, but could not stand himself for indulging in it.

Gradually, the night of sense made significant inroads: "The worldly activities in which I was engaged no longer satisfied me.... My quest for honor and wealth no longer enflamed me as before.... What really held me tightly bound, however, was my passionate need of woman" (8, 2).

Augustine had been able to let go practically everyone and everything except the emotional and sexual bond to certain women in his life, especially the mother of his son. Augustine desperately wanted conversion. He did everything he could to effect it. He sought guidance from Simplicianus, the spiritual father of Ambrose: "I hoped that if I discussed my struggles with him he might be able to show someone disposed as I was how to walk in your way, O Lord" (8, 1).

Augustine listened attentively to the words of Simplicianus and to the stories of conversion which he recounted: "I yearned to imitate" them, yet I remained "tied down not by irons outside myself, but by my own iron will.... I was still earthbound. I feared as much being freed from all my burdens as I ought to have feared being impeded by them" (8, 10-11).

"I was living my usual life with increasing anxiety" (8, 13). "I was certain that it was better to abandon myself to your love, O Lord, than to give in to my concupiscence. Yet, while your love attracted me to the point of almost winning its victory, cupidity was still alluring me and holding me in its fetters" (8, 12).

Augustine compares himself to a lazybones who lacks the courage to jump out of bed at the first sound of the bell. He lies there snug and comfortable under the blankets, saying: "Just one minute longer," and then lets that moment drag on and on. What could break this mood of hesitation and procrastination? He certainly could not (8, 12).

About this time Ponticianus, a North African compatriot, visited Augustine and his companion Alypius at their home in Milan. Ponticianus spoke to them enthusiastically of the monastic ideal, especially of the eremitical life and of the conversion experiences of several hermits who had been Roman officials. Their conversion had taken place after reading the *Life of St. Anthony*. Augustine was deeply touched and visibly moved by these stories. He wept at the wrenching anguish which resulted from the vehement pulling of his soul in opposing directions at the same time.

Still caught up "in these seething fevers of irresolution" (8, 20), Augustine retired to the solitude of a small garden adjacent to his residence to try to sort out his emotions and convictions. "Within myself, I kept repeating: Let it be done here and now. As I spoke, I felt that I was already advancing to the moment of decision. I was at the point of making it, yet I did not.... I tried again. I was almost there. I could all but taste it. Yet, I was not quite there. I was still vacillating between dying unto death and living unto life. Stronger in me was my customary worse than my untried better. The closer I came to becoming changed, the more terror it struck within me. My fear did not force me back or to the side. It rather held me in suspense" (8, 25).

"What gripped me ... were the alluring whisperings of my former mistresses tugging gently at the garment of my flesh: 'Are you going to send us away? From now on, we shall not be with you. For the rest of your life, such and such will not be permitted to you.' O my God, what suggestiveness and memories the phrase 'such and such' holds!... The whisperings continued, 'Do you really think that you can live without these things?'" (8, 26).

"The consternation within my heart boiled down to this: me against myself.... A flood of tears engulfed me... I prayed with the psalmist: How long, O Lord, how much longer? [Ps 6:4; 79:5].... Why not right now? Why not end my shame this very hour?" (8, 27-28).

"I kept repeating this out of the bitterest anguish of my contrite heart. And behold, I heard from a nearby house the voice of someone — whether a boy or a girl I do not know —chanting as it were and repeating over and over: *Tolle, lege* — take and read. . . .

"Having stemmed my torrent of tears . . . I hurried back to the place where Alypius was sitting. I grabbed the copy of Paul's epistles which I had left lying next to him. I opened it and read in silence the first passage on which my eyes fell: 'Not in merrymaking and drunkenness, not in orgies and sexual excesses, not in strife and jealously, but put on the Lord Jesus Christ. As for the flesh, take no account of its lusts' [Rm 13:13-14].

"I desired to read no further. Nor did I need to. Indeed, in that instant, with the termination of that sentence, all the darkness of doubt was dissipated by a light of peace flooding into my heart" (8, 29).

Augustine was baptized by Ambrose on the evening of April 24 or 25, 387 together with his son Adeodatus and his friend Alypius. As he testifies in the *Soliloquies*, however, the old-Augustine within him died very slowly after this conversion experience.

We do not want to clutter the power and the simplicity of this personal *metanoia* with a drawn out explanation. Let us point out just three striking features. *Mutatis mutandis*, these same features are also apparent in the following two examples of conversion. (1) God, and God alone, wrought this conversion immediately and directly. However, he used many human instruments, not the least of whom in Augustine's case was his mother Monica. (2) God, furthermore, used Augustine's resistance to peak his conversion. In other words, the more strongly Augustine resisted conversion, the more he yearned for it. If it had not cost him so much, it could not have been worth so much. A peak is measured by the abyss it crowns. (3) The external circumstance which triggered the actual breakthrough was one of the most banal events one can imagine: the shouting of a child next door, probably playing some game or other.

B. St. Teresa of Jesus (1515-1582)

At the time of her personal conversion, Teresa de Cepeda y Ahumada was about forty-two years old. She had been a nun at the convent of the Incarnation in Avila for almost twenty years.

Teresa describes the moment of her personal conversion in chapter 9 (pars. 1-9) of her *Life*. Some effects of this special grace were immediate. Others, however, God took two months to bring about. She treats these latter effects in chapters 23 (pars. 1-18) and 24 (pars. 1-8) of her *Life*.[1]

Teresa begins: "By this time in my life my soul had grown weary. Although I wanted to very much, I could not break the grip which my miserable habits had on me.

"One day, upon entering the oratory, I noticed a bust ... of Christ grievously wounded.... As I gazed at it, I was deeply moved at seeing him in such pain. So great was my distress when I realized how poorly I had repaid him for those wounds, that I felt my heart was breaking. I prostrated myself beside him, shedding floods of tears and begging him to give me the strength once and for all to never offend him again....

"I told him then and there that I was not going to get up off the floor until he granted my prayer. It did me a world of good, because from that moment I began to improve" (9, 1-3).

Teresa proceeds to describe her solitary prayer at the time of her conversion experience and immediately thereafter. She is clearly well into the transition from meditation to contemplation: "Since I could no longer discourse with my reason, I tried to represent Christ within myself" (9, 4).

An interesting stroke of providence occurred: "About this time I was given a copy of the *Confessions of St. Augustine*.... I have always had a special affinity with saints who

---

[1]Our paragraph numbers follow the 1984 Spanish Editorial de Espiritualidad critical edition of her *Obras Completas*. English translations differ with regard to paragraph enumerations.

had been sinners before the Lord turned them to himself" (9, 7).

Teresa concludes chapter 9 with this confession of her own: "I began to give myself more to prayer and became less involved in those things which did me harm. I still did not totally abandon these latter, but God kept on helping me turn from them. He was waiting for more preparedness on my part," before drawing out of me all the effects of this conversion experience.

Those "things" which did Teresa harm consisted in certain strong attachments to persons of both sexes inside and outside the convent, as well as the lack of intensity with which she had given herself to the daily exigencies of her religious vocation. She had cut many corners over those twenty years. What pained Teresa the most, however, was her infidelity to prayer.

In resuming the description of the aftermath of her conversion experience in the oratory, Teresa refers to it not only as marking a new chapter in her life, but as the beginning of a whole "new book. Until now the life I was describing was my own. But the life I have been living since ... is the life which God lives in me" (23, 1).

Teresa's prayer grew more contemplative by leaps and bounds during the next two months. At the time, she was sorely perplexed by some of the changes taking place: "It seemed to me that I was losing rather than gaining, because I did not properly understand at this time what God was accomplishing in me.... My fear increased to such a degree that I carefully sought out spiritual persons with whom I could discuss these matters" (23, 2-3).

The persons Teresa consulted were indeed very spiritual, but their advice on several specific points was inappropriate to her situation. She attributes part of the reason for this development to her own inability to describe adequately her prayer experiences. No doubt this is true. Yet, the other side of the coin is equally true: namely, some of these saintly men did not have sufficient theological background to be competent spiritual directors. Instead of listening attentively to the subtle and personalized movement of God within Teresa, some of these directors tried to impose on her their ready-made solutions. To further compound her anxiety, Teresa discovered that some of these persons had been talking about her behind her back, breaking the confidentiality which she had a right to expect.

"I was beset by trials on every side. I was like a woman who has fallen into a river. Whatever direction she tries to take, she is afraid of even greater danger, and yet she is almost drowning" (23, 12). The worst was still to come. One of her most trusted directors expressed his opinion that the source of her trouble was the devil. "This caused me such pain and distress that all I could do was weep" (23, 15).

At the depths of her despair, Teresa happened upon a line from 1 Corinthians (10:13): "God is faithful. He will not let you be tempted beyond what you are able to endure. On the contrary, he will give you a way out of every temptation." This passage afforded her much needed encouragement.

With this, Teresa resolved to make a detailed general confession to a Jesuit who had been recommended to her. In that celebration of the Sacrament of Reconciliation God drew out of her the final effects of her personal conversion: "After I had made this confession, my soul was so changed that I believed that there was nothing that I would not be prepared to do" or to undergo for Christ, "I began to have a new love for his most sacred humanity. My prayer henceforth began to take shape like a building upon solid foundations. I even began to grow fond of mortifications.... Any offense, however slight, against God pierced my soul to the quick. I could no longer tolerate all those superfluous things which had been such a part of my life. I could not rest until they were taken away" (24, 1-2).

Teresa's conversion also had a direct bearing on her many friendships: "Ever since that time, I have not been able to maintain a lasting relationship with anyone except those whom I believe love God and try to serve him. Furthermore, I could no longer be comforted by them nor entertain a particular affection for them. And it made no difference whether they were relatives or friends" (24, 6).

Teresa concludes the account of her personal conversion

with these pointed observations: "Since that day, I have remained so animated that I have given up everything for the sake of God. In that moment — and that is all it took —God completely changed me. . . . He set me free and gave me the strength to translate my resolution into practice. . . . Forever blessed be God, who in an instant gave me the freedom to attain what all my efforts for so many years were unable to accomplish" (24, 7-8).

C. St. Therese of the Child Jesus (1873-1897)

Marie Francoise Therese Martin was seven days short of her fourteenth birthday when her personal conversion occurred. It is commonly referred to as "the grace of Christmas."

"Yes, it was on December 25, 1886, that I received the grace to grow up. In effect, it was the grace of complete conversion."[2]

The events of that morning find their roots going back some ten years, to "the day of Mamma's death. . . . All the details of our dear mother's passing are still present to me. I remember especially well her last weeks on earth." Zelie Marie Martin died of cancer on August 28, 1877 in her forty-seventh year.

Therese was the youngest of nine in a deeply Christian and affectionate family. Therese was everybody's darling: "There is no denying it. The world treated me very well. Flowers were everywhere at my feet, and I had a happy disposition which made life pleasant for me" as well as for all those around me. "But now my soul had to begin a new period of its existence. I had to pass through the crucible of

---

[2]This and the following quotations are taken from what are called Therese's *Manuscripts autobiographiques*, the first of which was written in 1895 and dedicated to Mère Agnes de Jésus, her older sister and then Prioress of the Carmel of Lisieux. The translations are our own. See John Clark, trans., *Story of a Soul: The Autobiography of St. Therese of Lisieux*, ICS Publications, 1975, p. 30, 33-35, 97-98.

suffering from childhood on in order to become a more perfect offering to Jesus.

"This second period of my life — which was also the saddest of the three — lasted from the time I was four and a half to my fourteenth year.... It was only then that I really became a child again. That was also the moment when I began to enter into the serious phase of life. After Mamma's death my personality underwent a complete change.... I, who had been so vivacious and gregarious, was now a shy retiring little girl and oh, so hypersensitive. All it took to make me burst into tears was a simple glance from someone. I shunned people and their attention.... Yet, all this time I was surrounded by the most delicate tenderness on every side."

Emotionally, Therese went from bad to worse: frequent illnesses, "a mass of scruples," "the spoiled child of the family" and, after her sisters Pauline and Marie Louise entered Carmel, a loss of confidence in herself. "My touchiness in those days was insufferable. If I offended anyone whom I loved in the slightest way — even in the most accidental fashion — I wept uncontrollably.... Then, as soon as I began to cheer up, I would cry again for having cried in the first place. Nothing could appease me."

"Yes, I was still in diapers" at the age of thirteen. "God would have to perform a minor miracle to make me grow up.... The occasion he chose was Christmas."

Papa, Celine and I "had just returned home from midnight Mass.... As was our custom, I would go examine my Christmas slippers. We had loved this game so much in our childhood that Celine went on treating me like a baby.... Papa delighted too in seeing my happiness and in listening to my cries of glee as I took each surprise gift out of the magic slippers."

But that morning God had a surprise of his own. "Papa was tired after the midnight Mass, and the sight of my slippers by the fireplace irritated him. Just imagine how my heart was cut to the quick when I overheard him remark: 'Let's hope this is the last time that we have to go through this childishness.'" Of course, he had no idea that Therese was within earshot.

"I had been on my way upstairs at that moment to put away my hat. Celine, knowing how hypersensitive I was, saw the tears welling up in my eyes. She was in consternation.... 'Oh, Therese,' she pleaded, 'don't go down just yet. To look into your slippers right now will cause you too much pain,'" and ruin Christmas for the rest of us.

"But she did not know the Therese she was dealing with. Jesus had changed my heart" then and there. "Pushing back my tears, I turned and quickly went back downstairs. My heart was pounding. I fetched my slippers and placed them in front of Papa. As I joyfully took out my presents, you would have thought that I was as happy as a queen. Papa laughed. He was in good humor again. Celine could not believe her eyes.

"Yes, it was true. Little Therese had recovered the strength of soul which she had lost at four and a half. She would never lose it again.

"With this night of illumination, the third" and final "period of my life begins. It is the best of all, the richest in heavenly graces. In a single instant, Jesus accomplished what I had vainly tried to achieve these past ten years. I had tried, and that was enough for him."

Chapter 13

CELEBRATING PERSONAL CONVERSION

If the Eucharist as mystery celebrates sacramentally the contemplative dynamics of the threshold and stage of emergence, the Sacrament of Reconciliation is singularly suited to celebrate our personal conversion.

A. The Sacrament of Reconciliation, or of Conversion

The history of this sacrament is complex and controversial. There has even been considerable confusion as to what name to give it. Confession, penance, forgiveness, reconciliation, penitence, repentance, conversion? Each of these designations says something about the sacrament: the first two, more of its praxis; the latter five, more of its essence. Depending upon one's theological leanings and in which phase of historical development the sacrament is situated, one or other of these appellations can be appropriate.

Initially, this sacrament was scarcely distinguishable from adult Baptism. In the apostolic Church, what we call Baptism, Confirmation and Reconciliation were frequently synthesized into a simple sacramental act: the celebration of one's radical conversion to Christ. We think of the Ethiopian eunuch (Ac 8:36-39) and of St. Paul (Ac 9:17-18).

Later, as Baptism proper came to be administered earlier in life, Confirmation and Reconciliation took on new urgency and meaning. The commitment made in infant Baptism by one's godparents has to become personalized and intentionally reaffirmed in later life. Thus, the importance of Confirmation. Serious sin committed after Baptism and post-Baptismal conversion needs a sacramental expression of forgiveness and celebration. Thus, we receive the Sacrament of Reconciliation.

In the desert tradition the abbas and ammas tended to celebrate repentance privately and with a minimum of penitential acts. Most of the earliest monastic movements followed this practice which is based on an acute awareness of universal sinfulness coupled with a hesitancy to judge or condemn penitents, or *conversi* ("converted ones") as they were called in Latin. On the other hand, the rites of reconciliation of the established Church in the patristic era tended to be very public and were accompanied by severe and lengthy penances. Most of the early bishops followed this practice which was based on the idea of post-baptismal shipwreck. Public penance was a rescue operation to address what was considered an abnormal, scandalous situation. The rite of reconcilation was viewed so much as a second and last chance that it was often allowed only once in a lifetime and hence frequently put off until death was imminent.

These two traditions — the private, conversion-oriented approach of the desert fathers and mothers; and the public, penitentially-oriented rites of the established Church — evolved and eventually merged in the Middle Ages. Needless to say, the merger was fraught with a tension which is still not completely resolved. The Council of Trent canonized much of the sixteenth century scholastic theology and practice of Confession. Vatican II has taken a first step towards a renewal and deeper understanding of Reconciliation in the light of contemporary needs.[1]

[1]See Monika Hellwig, *Sign of Reconciliation and Conversion*, Michael Glazier, 1982.

The interior grace which this sacrament celebrates is first of all that of our repentance, of our conversion towards God. Then, as repentant sinners, it further celebrates our reconciliation with God, the Church and our neighbor. This sacrament is much richer in meaning and pastoral application than most people realize. Furthermore, it can have different meanings at diverse stages of our spiritual genesis. We wish to concentrate on one of these meanings at a most critical point of our spiritualization: the sacramental celebration of our personal conversion.

B. The Celebration of Conversion

In this section, we limit our discussion to biblical testimony on the subject.

The message of John the Baptizer leaves no room for doubt: *Metanoeite*, repent, be converted. God is already in our midst (Mt 3:2). Those committing themselves to this good news celebrated their conversion by receiving John's baptism of repentance. Jesus also received it. The dialogue between Jesus and John at the Jordan is revealing: "John tried to dissuade him, saying, 'I need to be baptized by you.' But Jesus replied, 'It is fitting that it be this way for now'" (Mt 3:14-15).

It was indeed fitting that Jesus celebrate in a visible manner his interior commitment to the public ministry which his Father had given him. In a very real sense he was celebrating his conversion: that is, the fact that he was (and had always been) totally turned to the Father and that his return to the Father was now in high gear.

Jesus began his public ministry with the same theme as John, only more urgently and more explicitly: "The time is now. God is already in your midst. *Metanoeite*, be converted and believe in the Gospel" (Mk 1:15). Then Jesus started forming a small community of converted believers. The account of their conversion and of its celebration is striking in its simplicity. Jesus "saw Simon and Andrew."

He said "Come, follow me.... And at once they left their nets and followed him" (Mk 1:16-18). The same pattern took place for James and John: "They left their father Zebedee in the boat with its crew and followed him" (Mk 1:20). Matthew's conversion is no less stunning: "Jesus saw him sitting in the tax collector's booth. He said, 'Follow me.' Matthew got up and followed him" (Mt 9:9).

Two details are common in these instances of *metanoia*: First, the perception of Jesus — "he saw them." He looked them straight in the eyes. He peered into the depths of their souls. And, second, he said: "Come, follow me." He called them to himself.

These apostles, in turn, do not say anything or ask any questions. According to the Synoptics, they do not pause to discuss the obvious: Who are you? What do you want? Where are we going? They do not even tidy up their affairs before departing. Their decisiveness of action was the exterior sign and celebration of their interior conversion. Simon and Andrew literally dropped their nets and went. James and John just walked away from their father who must have been dumbfounded. Matthew got up and left all that money sitting right there on the table.

The repentant woman celebrated her conversion by braving the ridicule of Simon the leper and by anointing Jesus's head with nard (Mk 14:3-9). Mary of Bethany celebrated her conversion by anointing Jesus's feet with perfume and wiping them with her hair (Jn 12:1-8). The Ethiopian eunuch celebrated his conversion by being baptized with water (Ac 8:36-39). Saul of Tarsus celebrated his conversion by allowing Ananias to lay hands on him and baptize him then and there (Ac 9:17-18).

No doubt the most expressive New Testament account of conversion and of its celebration is the parable of the wayward son and his loving father: Luke 15:11-32. The story is well known. Luke describes the moment of *metanoia* in these words: "Then, he came to his senses." The son's conversion is accompanied by deep contrition and repentance. He is not guilt-ridden in the emotional sense.

Feeling guilty as such is not Christian virtue, since it is predicated upon fear and trepidation. Contrition and compunction, on the other hand, certainly are Christian virtues. These are based on love and on the profound sorrow which result from having loved wrongly or not enough. Thus the converted son makes a firm resolve to do something concrete not only about his previous mode of life, but especially about his rebirth: "I will go back to my father."

The younger son's realization of his sin is also significant. He had sinned against both God and his family. Every sin —no matter how private — is a turning in upon oneself, hence also a turning away from God and humankind.

So, the son sets out to return: "But while he was still a long way off, his father saw him approaching and was filled with compassion. He rushed out to greet his son. He threw his arms around him and kissed him." The son tried to make a kind of oral confession, but the father cut him off in mid sentence. No need to dredge up all the past. What needs to be done is to celebrate this conversion: "Quick!" the father instructs his servants, "bring out the best robe... Put a ring on his finger and sandals on his feet.... Serve up the fatted calf. Let us celebrate. For this son of mine was dead and has risen. He was lost, but now is found."

Our personal conversion spontaneously seeks to be celebrated. This interior grace needs to be sacramentalized.

C. A Theological Reflection: The Sacrament of Conversion

The thoughts which follow represent a theological perspective different from the one ordinarily found in catechisms. This approach sheds particular light on the Sacrament of Reconciliation as a unique celebration not only of our personal conversion, but also of the other significant thresholds in our ongoing conversion process. There are admittedly other dimensions of this sacrament which apply to diverse aspects of spiritual development. We focus only upon this one, without denying the appropriateness of the others.

This theological perspective views the administration of the sacrament in question as co-ministry and therefore also as a concelebration. Matrimony is another co-ministered sacrament. In it, each spouse administers the sacrament one to the other. They concelebrate their marriage. The co-ministry in the sacrament of conversion, however, differs from that of marriage. The confessor[2] administers the sacrament to the penitent, and the penitent co-ministers the sacrament to him/herself. The confessor ministers by celebrating in an overt manner the conversion of the penitent with him/her and by imparting absolution in the name of Christ and the Church. With the confessor, the penitent co-ministers the celebration of his/her own conversion by bringing to the concelebrated event his/her repentance. Thus, the penitent not only receives something (e.g. absolution) but also does something. S/he actually celebrates sacramentally his/her own conversion.

In the case of matrimony the two participating spouses co-minister to each other in an identical fashion. In the case of the sacrament of conversion, the confessor and the penitent co-minister in different ways. The confessor concelebrates and absolves; the penitent concelebrates and receives this sign of God's loving forgiveness. Yet, the penitent does posit part of the sign, because part of the sacrament is the actual concelebration of his/her own conversion. A confessor is not essential for conversion as such to take place, since that transpires directly and immediately between God and the soul. However, a confessor is essential for the sacramental celebration of conversion, since it takes at least two actively participating persons to concelebrate. Moreover, the penitent cannot administer absolution to him/herself,

---

[2]We use the word "confessor" here because it is the most commonly accepted term to designate the duly authorized co-minister of this sacrament. We prescind from current disputes as to whether this co-minister can be someone other than a priest or a bishop.

even if he is a priest or bishop. This is so because absolution remains the prerogative of the other co-minister.

In this sacramental concelebration, the penitent represents him/ herself as repentant sinner. The confessor, on the other hand, represents the theandric nature of Christ: both human and divine. Since every sin is against God and society, an actual representative of both is necessary in the celebration of this sacrament. The confessor acts, therefore, in the name of God and humankind. Conversion of itself does not imply a previous turning away from God (as with Jesus and his mother Mary). In our case, however, personal conversion always implies repentance for actual sinfulness (1 Jn 1:8-10).

The thrust of the sacrament is not backward, but forward towards God. Because we are so radically turned towards God, we must be turned away from whatever is not of him. The thrust of the sacrament is towards reconciliation with God, the Church and our neighbor, regardless of our sinfulness.

According to this theological perspective, the sacramental concelebration presupposes the *metanoia* of the penitent. The sacrament thus affirms and confirms the conversion which has already taken place. The effectiveness of the sacrament consists in absolution from ecclesiastical censure as well as in the confirmation of what God has forgiven and turned towards himself.

The special grace of the sacrament in this view is personal and ecclesial ratification of the penitent's conversion, together with the launching forward of that faith commitment for the rest of the penitent's life.

D. Pastoral Implications of this Theological Perspective

Certain pastoral consequences follow from the foregoing theological reflection.

(1) The most obvious consequence is that this sacrament

is uniquely suited to celebrate the moment of our personal conversion. Naturally, there may not be a confessor immediately available when God directly effects our *metanoia*. Nonetheless, we quite normally want (even need) to celebrate sacramentally that singular grace sooner or later, one way or another. St. Teresa of Jesus took two months before celebrating hers.

(2) *Metanoia* is an ongoing process both before and after the moment of personal conversion. Even though that moment is unique in our individual salvation history, there are usually other significant thresholds of conversion both before and after it. This sacrament is especially well suited to celebrate them as well.

(3) This brings us to the question of the optimum frequency of the sacrament. Since most of us do not experience a breakthrough in conversion every Friday afternoon at three o'clock, it stands to reason that strictly routine confession is of little spiritual value. We celebrate this sacrament when we need to in a spirit of true repentance, not as a panacea against guilt trips or guilt complexes.

Since the penitent in this view is a co-minister and a concelebrant, the subjective element of this sacrament is of special importance. There is no a priori optimum regarding frequency. The conversion process of some persons may require very frequent celebration of this sacrament at certain phases of interior development. In this sense, what have been commonly called "devotional confessions" and "regular confessions" may not only be useful, but also needed. Moreover, there are other dimensions of this sacrament which we have not discussed here. These other dimensions may predicate greater frequency as well. In any case, the special grace of this sacrament is not linked to quantity of times, but uniquely to the quality of repentance.

(4) This theological perspective in no way militates against early catechesis and celebration of the sacrament. On the contrary, it adds new light and urgency to the education of very young Christians regarding their participation in this sacrament. Our conversion process begins

even before we are born. Therefore, it is never too early to begin helping a child appreciate the sacramental concelebration of the significant moments of that process.

(5) What light does this view shed on the question of examination of conscience? The more God draws us from discursive prayer into contemplation, the less meaningful particular and general examens become. The reason for this mutation is simple. The more contemplative God makes us, the more explicitly loving we remain towards him and towards our neighbor. The slightest deviation from that love stands out like a sore thumb. We recognize at once our need for reconciliation. We could not hide from our sinfulness, if we tried.

Nevertheless, on specific occasions even someone advanced in contemplative prayer can be moved to examine his/her conscience. This examination is most Christianly performed by following the Beatitudes (Mt 5:3-11) and *Agape* (1 Cor 13, especially 4-7). Whatever method of examination is used, however, the most important purpose of any examen is to arrive at a better understanding of the causes of our sinfulness. Our "sins" are but symptoms of a much deeper problem. It is that problem which above all needs addressing and confessing. When we visit our doctor, s/he is not overly concerned with our aches and pains. The doctor tries to pierce beyond these symptoms and treat their cause.

(6) What is the best way — format, as it were — to sacramentally celebrate our conversion? The best way is whatever manner expresses most authentically the interior reality which is concelebrated by both the confessor and the penitent. This can range from a detailed "general confession" to a simple gesture of repentance. What is important is that the manner we choose be sacramentally meaningful to both concelebrants.

Chapter 14

CONTINUED CONVERSION : THE LIGHT AND NIGHT OF SPIRIT

The threshold of emergence ushers us into the contemplative phase of our spiritual genesis. This phase intensifies progressively until we reach our personal death, wherein our entire life is epitomized in the simple act of complete loving surrender to God.

The threshold of personal conversion synthesizes all that precedes it and catapults us into the rest of our mortal life. Sometimes this conversion takes place on the proverbial deathbed, and occasionally only in death itself. Once in a while, we are privileged to witness it taking place in a loved one. At other times we can only believe that our compassionate Father brought about this conversion in his infinite mercy and wisdom, without anyone being able to notice it.

For many of us, however, our personal conversion occurs well before death. What then do we have to look forward to while we await our transition into eternity? The response is universally applicable: further emergence with Christ in the twofold form of more advanced contemplation and night of spirit.

For some people, God draws out the initial stages of their interior development over virtually an entire lifetime. In these cases, he condenses into a few days, into a few moments or even in the instant of death itself the later stages of adult spiritual genesis. It all takes place for each of us in God's time and in his way. The Lord alone knows why he works as he does and how he makes up in intensity what is lacking in duration.

The older we grow and the more spiritually mature we become, however, the more the two arms of God's all-embracing love tighten around us. As they tighten, we are more transformed in him and that transformation in turn purges us all the more intensely.

A. Purgatory

Our mortal life is really our purgatory, or at least a major portion of it. What is still unconsumed by God's transforming love at death is totally consumed by the unlimited personal encounter with divine love in death itself. The processes which we experience quantitatively and successively in space and time are experienced in a purely qualitative manner in death. All our earthly points of reference are instantaneously transcended in death. Of course, our ontological limitations remain in eternity. We are still creatures with individual personalities, etc. But all our mortal limitations — space, time, motion, etc. — are removed by the act of death itself.

Our personal death occurs when our past has completely exhausted our future, and our entire life is now. Stripped of all our mortal limitations, we then fully encounter God who is pure Love (1 Jn 4:8, 16), pure Light (1 Jn 1:5) and pure Spirit (Jn 4:24). Such divine love and light are engendered within us that their sheer intensity purges us in that instant of whatever is not transformable in God. In the moment of personal death, God's love so divinizes us that that very love consumes everything in us which has not yet been spiritualized. Death is the point where the two arms of God's all-embracing love meet, and our whole being and life end up fully transformed in God with nothing left to be purged.

We sometimes hear the saying: Those whom God loves more, he makes suffer more. Depending on the tone of voice and look of the eye, this saying can be uttered in frustration, anger, tongue in cheek, love, faith or wonderment. The truth of the matter is that God's love does purify us to the utmost. As Teilhard de Chardin so aptly puts it: "If being united means in every case being changed and dying at least partially in/to what one loves, then this being annihilated in the other must be all the more complete the more we give ourselves to the One who is greater than ourselves. We can set no limits to the uprooting which is part and parcel of our journey in God."[1]

God's love is transforming, not punitive. It lifts us up, not beats us down. Death is directed towards resurrection and eternal life, not extinction. Our cross is unto glory, not expiation as such. St. John of the Cross hits the nail on the head: "Even though this blessed night darkens the spirit, it does so only to impart light in all things. And even though it humbles us and reveals our miseries, it does so only to exalt us. And even though it empties us of all our attachments and natural affections, it does so only that we may reach forward divinely to enjoy and take pleasure in everything in heaven and on earth, all the while preserving a general freedom of spirit in them all."[2]

There is nothing more crucifying than love, because there is nothing more self-emptying than love. God so loved the world that he gave his only Son (Jn 3:16). Jesus so loved each one of us that he gave himself (Jn 13:1), sharing the Spirit of truth and love with us (Jn 14:16-17; 15:26).

Yes, indeed, we are sinners. Moreover, sin and its consequences do enter deeply into the mystery of our need for purgation. However, the basic purpose of purification goes much deeper than personal sin. Jesus and his mother had to suffer and die because of the exigencies of transforming love. Not everything that needs purifying is necessarily of a moral order (or immoral, as the case may be). Our natural, physical, emotional, psychological limitations are also transformed, and hence necessarily purified.

[1] *D. Milieu*, p. 88. See *Receptivity*, pp. 48-49, 93-97.
[2] *Night*, II, 9, 1. See *Night*, II, 16, 7; *Receptivity*, p. 48-49.

The intensity of God's light has a direct bearing on the intensity of our darkness. On the one hand, the more God makes us conscious of his love, the more we appreciate the utter incomprehensibility and transcendence of his love. On the other hand, the more God transforms us in himself, the more that transformation reveals our poverty and weaknesses. Even God's immanence is transcendent. His light reveals who and what we really are and are not. All this is experienced as darkness to our minds and as aridity to our emotions.

Following the threshold which we have termed personal conversion, most people experience a period of relative tranquility. The ongoing process of transforming union continues, and so does that of purification. Yet, it is more the joy of growth in Christ which dominates our consciousness than the pain of purgation.

This perception is due not only to the fact that God may be giving us a respite, but also to the fact that the threshold of personal conversion is itself such a liberation that no suffering ever again affects us emotionally and psychologically in quite the same way. Thus, even though the night of spirit is objectively more intense than much of the purgation preceding personal conversion, many persons do not experience it as emotionally traumatic as those earlier phases of the night. In a certain sense, the worst is yet to come after personal conversion, since we still have the night of spirit and death to undergo. However, in another sense, the worst is now behind us. For the increasing awareness of God's transforming love is so dominant that we joyfully look forward to the more definitive liberation of the night of spirit and personal death. St. John of the Cross powerfully expresses these sentiments in his poem: *Vivo sin vivir . . . muero porque no muero*: "I live without living . . . and I die because I do not die."

The interior throes leading up to personal conversion are already a participation in the night of spirit. Yet the more advanced dimensions of this purgation follow our conversion experience. And these more advanced dimensions are indeed very dark and painful.

Thus, frequently the threshold of personal conversion occurs between the onset of the night of sense and the full brunt of the night of spirit. John describes that intervening breakthrough as though "one had broken out of a confining prison."[3] Enjoying this freedom, we relish the new depths of contemplation which God bestows. We are drawn forward in God ever more decisively.

Eventually, however, the relative calm following our conversion gives way to the full impact of the night of spirit.

B. *The Night of Spirit in General*

"This dark night is an influence of God from within the soul which purges it of its ignorances and imperfections, whether they are habitual, natural or spiritual. Contemplatives call this influence of God 'contemplation'.... In this contemplative night God secretly instructs us in the perfection of love, without our doing anything or even understanding what is taking place. This divine contemplation is God's loving wisdom. As such, it produces two principal effects in us: It purges and illumines us, thereby preparing us for union of love with God himself."[4]

There is a world of difference between the night of sense for beginners in contemplation (*principiantes*) and the night of spirit for those more advanced (*aprovechados*). It can be compared to "the difference between pruning a branch and pulling up a root or between washing out a fresh stain and scrubbing out an old one which is deeply embedded."[5]

The night of sense and the night of spirit are in reality but one night of the soul in successive stages. They may be compared to sundown and midnight. The night of sense is more accurately a kind of curbing and bridling of our passions rather than a purgation as such. This is so because "all our sensory imperfections and disorders find their root

---

[3]*Night*, II, 1, 1. See *Receptivity*, pp. 32-36.
[4]*Night*, II, 5, 1. See *Receptivity*, pp. 36-41.
[5]*Night*, II, 2, 1.

and strength in the spirit." Therefore, "until the spirit is sufficiently purged, the sensate aspect of the human person cannot be thoroughly purified. In the night of the spirit then, both our sensate and spiritual dimensions are purged together, since one is never truly purified without the other."[6]

The phrase "night of spirit" thus denotes a radical transformation and purification of our whole being. This purgation directly attains both our perceptible or sensory aspects and our deepest and most spiritual core: that which constitutes our personhood as such. God effects this night in and through all the concrete circumstances of our daily lives. Everyone goes through the whole night, for each person must die in order to be raised deified.

The same divine flame of contemplative love unites us to God and purges all that is un-God-like in us. It is because we are being so completely transformed that we are being so intensely purified: like gold in a crucible. In the latter phases of the night of spirit, we have the impression that we are being emptied to the point of death. Indeed, our inner struggle at this time resembles, and in some instances actually coincides with, the grieving process which we undergo in approaching our physical death. Normally, the grieving person struggles with denial and isolation, anger and resentment, bargaining and confusion, depression and trepidation before being drawn into true acceptance and resignation.

"The soul feels itself melting away. It is being torn apart at the seams by a cruel spiritual death." It is coming unglued. "We have the impression of having been swallowed by a beast and of being digested in the darkness of its belly, suffering the anguishes of Jonah (2:1). We must remain in this sepulchre of dark death in order to receive the spiritual resurrection for which we yearn."[7] St. Therese of the Child Jesus describes her experience of the night of spirit in very similar terms in her final autobiographical manuscript writ-

---

[6]*Night*, II, 3, 1-2.
[7]*Night*, II, 6, 1.

ten just four months before her death. Therese, of course, expands on these images in her own inimitable way.[8]

This fire of divine love causes in us an overwhelming experience of inner poverty. From the deepest recesses of our being, this flame drives up into consciousness the awareness of our weaknesses and sinfulness, which hitherto we had successfully kept hidden behind defense mechanisms. As God's light pierces through these defenses and his love consumes them, we encounter our limitations as never before. We have the impression that we are worse than ever: more lustful, more irascible, more resentful, more selfish. The truth of the matter is that we have always been that way, but we could not bring ourselves to admit it. Now that we can no longer hide from our true selves, we are much better off spiritually.

In the midst of all this pain, anxiety and darkness we paradoxically realize that God's love is not punitive. It is not of itself afflictive. Whatever affliction we suffer derives from our self-centeredness. "There is nothing in contemplation that can of itself cause pain. On the contrary, God's activity within us causes intense peace and delight.... What makes us suffer is rather the weakness and imperfection of our interior dispositions. These render us unfit to receive God himself within us."[9]

God is not to blame. We are. "How amazing and pitiful it is that our weakness and impurity are such that the gentle and tender touch of God should feel so heavy and contrary to us. The hand of God does not press down or weigh upon us. It only touches us and does so mercifully."[10]

The fire of divine love would not be oppressively experienced if it had nothing to purge. Once we are sufficiently purified, our sensations of affliction cease, and only the blessings of the night remain.

At the core of all this purgation is the fact that the Holy Spirit is enkindling greater love in us. During the more

---

[8]See John Clark, trans., *Story of a Soul*, ICS Publications, 1975, pp. 210-214.

[9]*Night*. II, 9, 11.

[10]*Night*, II, 5, 7. See *Receptivity*, pp. 48-49.

intense throes of the night, we do not, however, advert to this truth. Our surface powers of concentration are too captivated by our pain and confusion. Yet every once in a while, God does give us a break: "It is as though a blacksmith draws the iron out of the furnace in order to size up the work which he is doing. When God does this, we perceive within ourselves the good which we could not see while the work was going on."[11]

After each such period of relief, however, we are put back into the furnace and are purified more intensely and more interiorly than before. But this time the fire penetrates into the more intimate, subtle and spiritual recesses of our heart. This interplay between purification, relief and more intense purification finds a parallel in the life of Jesus. Luke (together with Matthew and Mark) situates the transfiguration of Jesus between two prophecies of his passion which he uttered on his way up to Jerusalem. The actual Greek word is "transformation": "He was transformed (*metemorphothe*) before them" (Mt 17:2; Mk 9:2). Jesus' humanity —and a fortiori that of Peter, James and John — needed this unusual experience of his divinity's transforming love before he could face the deeper purification of his passion.

Even though a state of anguish may quickly return, when we see ourselves so richly blessed during these intervals of relief we frequently assume that our trials are over. This is typified by the naively euphoric reaction of Peter at the transfiguration. But as Luke (9:33) notes: "He did not know what he was saying." More often, however, even in these times of surface relaxation we cannot escape the subtle awareness that there still remains much incompleteness to our peace and joy. "Until our spiritual purification is perfected, this communication of God which we experience as so relieving is rarely so intense as to conceal completely from us the roots which have yet to be purged. We continue to realize that there is something which we lack within ourselves or that there is still much to be done."[12]

[11]*Night*, II, 10, 6.
[12]*Night*, II, 7, 6.

Therefore, we usually do not fully enjoy these respites. We intuit that an enemy continues to lurk within. Although hushed and asleep, it will awaken and plunge us once more into spiritual darkness. "Just when we feel most secure and least expect it, we are dragged down and immersed again in another and more intense affliction. It is more severe, dark and miserable than the previous one. This renewed affliction, moreover, usually lasts longer than the first. Thus, we begin to fear all over again that we have lost God's blessings forever."[13]

In the night of spirit then, the fire of divine love within us transforms and purifies us in a progressively more interior manner. On a perceptible level, we experience periods of more and more intense trial. These are interspersed with periods of increased peace, joy and tranquillity. God keeps us in this night until our spirit is humbled, mellowed and purified. We thus grow so sensitive, simple and pure that we become one with the Spirit of God. According to the intensity of union to which God desires to raise us and in accordance with the degree of our imperfection, the night of spirit is of greater or lesser intensity and duration. Yet, if it is to attain the core of our being, it must be very intense and can last for years.

C. Signs and Conditions of Authenticity

What principles do spiritual directors follow in order to discern the authenticity of the night of spirit in their directees? Since the night of spirit is a more intense prolongation of the night of sense, the same basic signs and conditions apply in both phases of the same night of the soul. Therefore, we now extend the principles which we enunciated in chapter 8 to the question at hand.

The first sign and condition indicating that God is drawing us through the night of spirit is an ever deepening experience of aridity: dryness across the board. This

---

[13] *Night*, II, 7, 6.

increased aridity directly affects the quality of our personal commitment to Christ. It sorely tests the quality of our faith in Jesus. These trials of faith are similar to, but more intense than, those storms of the spirit of dizziness which characterize the night of sense.

The second sign and condition authenticating the night of spirit is increased spiritual anxiety and restless questioning regarding all that is taking place. We fear that we are backsliding, almost to the point of despair. Thus, the quality of our hope in God is tested and purified. These anxieties are akin to, but more forceful than, the storms of the spirit of blasphemy which are associated with the previous phase of the night.

The third sign and condition discernible in the night of spirit centers around our love of God, our *agape*. Contemplative prayer is firmly established in us by this time. We are well aware of an ever increasing need for prolonged silence and solitude. Yet, amid this vibrant outpouring of love for God, we experience violent surges of the spirit of fornication. These can be even more vehement and confounding than those of the night of sense.

It is evident, therefore, that the most operative of God's gifts to us at this stage of spiritual genesis are faith, hope and love, the greatest of these, of course, being love (1 Cor 13:13). Our emergence is in its final stages, even if we still have many more years to live. God's transforming love is boring into the very core of our being, purging out the deepest and also the last vestiges of self-centeredness. We feel like the substrata of the earth as the oil rig above pounds away more and more feverishly on its way to pay dirt. We wonder if the drilling will ever cease. And all the while, God's activity is piercing through to the very heart of our being.

The next three chapters take up successively how God's transforming and purifying activity within us both increases and purifies our faith, hope and love during the night of spirit.

Chapter 15

THE LIGHT AND NIGHT OF FAITH

In its biblical sense, faith is a radical commitment to the person of Jesus Christ. It is infinitely more than an intellectual assent to certain dogmas or beliefs. Faith is not primarily *about* some-thing, but rather *in* some-One: "Do you believe in the Son of Man?" (Jn 9:35). "The life I now live, I live in faith: faith in Christ Jesus" (Ga 2:20).

Faith is a commitment of that which is deepest, most ineffable and most mysterious in us to what is deepest, most ineffable and most mysterious in the person of Jesus. Thus, by its very nature faith leaves us in darkness, since it pertains to those depths of ourselves and of God which are entirely beyond the grasp of our intellect, emotions and imagination.

Faith is interpersonal, because not only do we believe in God, but also God believes in each of us. He has committed himself to us as unique individual persons. He is committed specifically to our personal salvation and transformation in himself. His commitment to us is the source of our ability to become committed to him.

Faith as interpersonal commitment is a dynamic process. In the night of spirit, faith calls forth the gradual and progressive surrender of ourselves to God in hope and love. Faith denotes our immediate and direct abandonment to God in unmitigated risk and mystery. This attitude is evident in Jesus' final prayer from the cross: "Father, into your hands, I commit my spirit" (Lk 23:46).

A. Faith and the Night

In relation to the night of spirit, faith is a myriad of paradoxes.

Faith is both the cause of the night as well as the only guide through it. St. John of the Cross captures this contrast and interplay in stanzas 3-5 of his poem *In a Dark Night*:

> In this blessed night,
> In secret, when no one saw me
> Nor could I see anything,
> Without other light or guide
> Save that which burned in my heart.
>
> This guided me
> More surely than the light of noonday
> To a place where he awaited me
> — he whom I knew so well —
> A place where no one appeared.
>
> Oh night that guides me!
> Oh night more lovely than the dawn!
> Oh night that united
> Beloved with lover,
> Lover transformed in Beloved!

Although it has an obscuring effect on our powers of perception, faith of itself is divine light. Indeed, it is pure light and pure gift. Faith illumines, however, by way of kenosis; that is, by way of emptying. It teaches us who God is in reality by causing us to experience who he is not and who we are not. By faith we learn to know by unknowing.

This paradoxical knowing by unknowing comprises two dimensions. (1) The brilliance of its illumination unmasks our many illusions about God and ourselves. (2) Faith furthermore reveals to us that God in himself is infinitely beyond all that we perceive of him. Regardless of the sublimity of our experience of him or the accuracy of our knowledge of his love, mercy, forgiveness, etc., God remains transcendent. He is always other not only in relation to what we mistakenly imagine him to be, but also in relation to what we perceive him in truth to be. Consequently, in order to encounter the real God in faith we have to pass beyond all our own ways, logic, concepts, images, reasonings, feelings and imaginings. Only thus can we hope to journey in the dark night/light of faith.

Faith increases in proportion to the darkness and aridity of the night. This does not mean that darkness and aridity themselves increase faith. Only God bestows faith and only he can produce an increase of his absolutely free gift. Nonetheless, darkness and aridity are necessary conditions, if faith is to increase. Why? For this reason: By letting the darkness and aridity of the night produce their purgative effects, God removes even the possibility of our clinging to anything or anyone other than himself. Apparently abandoned by all others, we are thus disposed to abandon ourselves more deeply in faith to God himself.[1]

In the night of spirit, God radically purifies our faith by stripping away certain supports, attachments and defense mechanisms. Yet, rather than recognizing the emergence of a more qualitative life in faith, our general impression is frequently that of being remiss in faith or of possibly losing it altogether. The disparity between the interior reality and our surface perceptions becomes especially noticeable in three areas: commitment, values and self-identity.

B. Commitment

Paradoxically, growth in faith coincides with increased anguish and painful questioning with regard to our personal commitment to Christ Jesus. This frightful searching can be expressed in many ways: Do I truly believe in the Lord? How do I know for sure that I believe in him? Do I really desire to believe in him? How much of myself am I willing to

---

[1]See *Canticle*, 12, 1-9; *Receptivity*, pp. 49-53, 97-101; *Ascent*, II, *passim*.

give back to God? Considering the possibly limitless consequences of a deeper commitment, how open to God am I willing to be? Where are you, Lord? What is your will? Am I really serving you? Am I in fact doing your will? Am I letting your will be done in and through me?

This anguished questioning arises not only with respect to the interpersonal commitment itself, but also in regard to every aspect of our Christian life. We are no longer content with pat answers as to the meaning of the sacraments, the value of religious life, the nature of the Church, etc. Through the night of spirit, we are becoming emancipated Christians, and we need to reexamine all the tenets of our belief in the light of this newly intensified and purified faith.

This reexamination is usually very disconcerting. In the actual raising of these questions, we experience ourselves being stripped of and having to let go the comfort and security of familiar answers and practices. While this searching is going on, we are frequently bombarded by storms similar to, but stronger than, the spirit of dizziness characteristic of the night of sense. We crave to know where we are and where we are going. We are tempted to seek reassurance in clear-cut answers, but there are none. We are left reeling in terrifying uncertainty and anxiety. Many times, we are unable to find support in any person or advice.

Deeper faith emerges out of this anguished searching. Painful questioning, with its ensuing darkness, is the milieu in which God increases within us the gift of faith. This is so because the searching and questioning prod us to let go all that is familiar and observable. Then we can plunge more intensely into the unknown, into the mystery of God's love. The Lord uses these anxieties as a means of stripping us of anything which we might cling to and which might thus impede our forward thrust and absolute trust. We remain in the darkness of faith, knowing by unknowing.

Thomas Merton's prayer of abandonment captures many of these sentiments:

> My Lord God, I have no idea where I am going.
> I do not see the road ahead of me.

I cannot know for certain where it will end.
Nor do I know myself, and the fact that I think
I am following your will does not mean that
I am actually doing so.
But I believe that the desire to please you does in
fact please you.
And I hope I have that desire in all that I am doing.
I hope that I will never do anything apart from that
desire.
And I know that if I do this you will lead me by the
right road, though I may know nothing about it.
Therefore I will trust you always though I may seem
to be lost and in the shadow of death.
I will not fear, for you are ever with me, and you will
never leave me to face my perils alone.[2]

In discerning the authenticity of the night of spirit, directors have to discover the source of the anxieties which their directees experience. It is one thing to fear losing one's faith, while in fact growing in virtue. It is quite another thing to lose one's mind. A wise spiritual director is needed in the first instance, a competent psychologist in the second. When God is the source, all our restless searching constitutes a positive sign of a vibrant, deepening faith. God is calling us to let go all the trappings which we imagine to be faith.

If the directee is authentically undergoing the night of spirit, the director will perceive that despite the intensity of the struggle the directee continues to abandon him/herself ever more consciously to God. The two qualities of acquiescence in mystery and profound acceptance of God as he really is increase through all this upheaval.

The director will also see within the directee both a grateful recognition of the faith which s/he has already received and a humble realization of a lack of faith. The prayer of the epileptic demoniac's father — "Lord, I do believe, help my unbelief" (Mk 9:24) — arises out of the depths of an anguished, yet grace-filled heart.

[2]*Thoughts in Solitude*, Doubleday Image Book #D 247, 1968, p. 81.

C. Reevaluation

The system of values and the responsibilities which flow out of our personal commitment to God also undergo a thorough shake-up in the night of spirit.

By the onset of this phase of the night, the values which took on such importance at the beginning of the night of sense have already been integrated into our lifestyle. These values include: simplicity of demeanor, poverty of spirit, love of solitude, service to others for the sake of Christ, material frugality, etc. In the night of spirit, however, we experience increasing aridity with respect to these values as they were previously concretized. They seem to be drying up and withering away. My service to others, for example, may still be meaningful to them, but to my emotions and perceptions that ministry is imbued with an overwhelming sense of futility and uselessness. I have to almost make myself answer the door. I can make no sense out of living this way. Time off or vacations do not help either. My previous values, as they were lived before, can no longer make life meaningful in the present. Ministerial burn-out can produce the same reactions. However, when God's transforming activity within us is the source of this change, growth in faith is discernible.

When we are growing in faith through this intense aridity, we consistently live and act more out of Christian convictions and principles than from feelings, likes and dislikes. The indwelling Trinity becomes our driving force and sole motivation. In our daily life, we strive for utmost fidelity even in our most banal, insignificant and minute responsibilities. We do whatever we do specifically for God. Since we can no longer get anything out of our activities for ourselves, we pursue them solely for him. We persevere in our commitments not so much because they are a value to us or even to others. We persevere mainly because of God himself.

Therefore, our reevaluation at this point is not so much in terms of searching for new values to replace the old ones, but rather of letting the motivation behind those same values be transformed. At this stage of development, we attain God less through our values — no matter how excellent they remain. We are now communing more directly with God in himself. In a sense, our values have lost their luster because God has replaced them with himself.

D. Self-Identity

As we are drawn through the night of spirit, we seem not only to be losing our way (and perhaps our mind!), but our self-identity as well. As God's light strips us of our deeply embedded attachments to our own opinions, desires, experiences, feelings and viewpoints, we find that what we had called our "self" is slipping away. It is very difficult to know ourselves by unknowing. All former certitudes and securities dissipate. We really have no idea who we are or where we are headed in terms of any experiential framework. In reality, however, we are living out one of the most exigent logia of the Gospel: "Whoever loses his/her life for my sake will find it" (Mt 10:39). Thus, we are not actually losing our self-identity. We are losing our old self, our surface self, our immature self, our self-centeredness. In so doing, we discover our true self in Christ.

Commitment of our whole self to Christ in faith requires death to self. True life in Christ flows out of this death: "The one who believes in me will live, even though s/he dies ... and whoever lives and believes in me will never die" (Jn 11:25-26).

By losing our way we enter more deeply in faith upon the Way who is Christ himself (Jn 14:6). No matter how sublime our knowledge or appreciation of God may be, he is always infinitely beyond it. "On this road" to transforming union "to lose one's way is to enter into the way. In other words, to pass on to the goal and to leave one's way is to enter into that which has no way at all: namely, God. For the soul who arrives at this stage no longer has any ways or methods of its own ... though it contains within itself all ways after the manner of one who possesses nothing yet possesses all things [2 Co 5:10]."³

Although the light of faith illumines more clearly who God is not and who we are not, we sometimes come away with the impression that we are aimlessly lost, rather than lost in Christ. We cringe at the very real possibility of losing not just ourselves but God as well. Paradox of all paradoxes! This very impression constitutes an essential sign of spiritual progress. This experience of lostness is the normal reaction of a mortal creature having come into direct and immediate contact with the living God. We simply cannot contain him or his love for us. His light overwhelms all our powers of knowing both him and ourselves. Thus, these powers are left in darkness, while our true self is being bathed in unquenchable light.

There exists another positive sign value in our painful impression of being lost. If we did not love God so much, we would not care whether or not we had lost him. We would still be very fearful at the prospect of having lost our way or our self. Yet, if the person of Christ were not really the center of our lives, we would not be perturbed at being separated from him.⁴ Therefore, the fact that we are so anguished over the situation as we perceive it, is an essential sign that God has already found us and has a firm grip on us. This is so even though we have not yet found him to a degree sufficient to assuage our anxieties. However, that too will come when he has made us ready.

³*Ascent*, II, 4, 5.
⁴See *Contemplation*, pp. 65-68.

Chapter 16

THE LONGING AND NIGHT OF HOPE

Profound faith in God and profound hope in God are hardly distinguishable from each other on most accounts. Deep within the human person all the theological virtues ultimately dovetail into one: *agape*, love. "Love believes all, hopes all" (1 Co 13:7).

Normally, we associate faith with light and commitment. The night of faith evokes darkness and anxiety. Usually, we associate hope with longing and straining forward. The night of hope evokes fear and emptiness. Faith is towards God in himself, but as already within us. Hope is towards God in himself, but as not yet fully attained.

In reaction to the intense aridity which permeates all aspects of our lives, we suffer many grave doubts and misgivings, much anxiety and fear. This situation ultimately confronts us with two possible options — either hope in God or despair.

There are several important dimensions of Christian hope with reference to the night of spirit: its relationship to memory and forgetfulness, its restlessness and emptiness, the impact of trust and fear, and the signs of authentic hope.

A. Memory and Forgetfulness

Today there is much talk about the healing of memories. St. John of the Cross consistently speaks of hope in relation to *memoria*. For John *memoria* is rich in meaning.

Memory is the faculty or interior capacity which contains and stores all natural knowledge obtained through our external senses (seeing, touching, hearing, etc.) as well as through our interior senses (feeling, imagining, knowing, etc.). Our memory furthermore harbors our knowledge of God attained through meditation. It contains also our experience of good and evil. It gives a sense of continuity to our past, present and future.[1]

However, for John of the Cross memory comprises an affective dimension as well. It denotes the yearning of the heart for Truth and Goodness at their source. Memory propels us forward in our insatiable quest for God in himself. In this sense, John evokes the Augustinian meaning of *memoria*, described so poignantly by the Bishop of Hippo in his *Confessions* (1, 1): "You have made us for yourself alone, O Lord, and our heart is restless until it rests in you."

Thus, hope heals our memory by irrevocably pointing us beyond our past and present preoccupations to the fullness of participation in God: "The sufferings of this present life can in no way be compared with the glory which is awaiting us" (Rm 8:18). Yet, in healing us of our introspective concerns — this hurt, that pain; this death, that rejection; this resentment, that contradiction — evangelical hope wounds us even more deeply. It wounds us positively by awakening us to the insatiability of our appetite for consummate transforming union in love with God.[2] This is ultimately what "forgetfulness" — whether of self or of anything created — means in the spirituality of John of the Cross. His four-line poem *The Summa of Perfection* epitomizes this thought:

Olvido de lo criado,	Forgetfulness of creatures,
Memoria del Criador,	Memory of our Creator,
attención a lo interior	Attentiveness to what is spiritual,
y estarse amando al Amado.	And remaining loving our Beloved.

---

[1]See *Ascent*, III, 2-14.
[2]See *Receptivity*, pp. 27-31; *Canticle*, 6, 6-7.

God's healing of our memories, therefore, ultimately brings upon us the full brunt of the night of spirit.

B. *Restlessness and Emptiness*

Forgetfulness of self or of anything created means realizing our inability to be fully satisfied with anything or anyone other than God in himself. Hope, therefore, pertains to that which we have not yet attained. "By hope we are saved. Yet hope which is seen is not really hope, because no one hopes for what s/he already sees. But when we hope for what we do not see, we yearn for it with patience" (Rm 8:24-25).

The New Testament word for hope is *elpis* which translates the Hebrew *batah* (to cling to, to rely upon, to trust or confide in) and *qavah* (to wait for, to hope in, to be strong). Hebrew has no neutral concept of expectation. Its object is either good or bad. Therefore, expectation elicits either hope or fear.

Hope is not a consoling dream that whisks away our present troubles. It is trust and confidence in God, in his providence and in his purpose. Thus, we cannot really trust riches (Ps 52:9), our own righteousness or that of others (Ez 33:13), anything human (Jer 17:5), or even our religious inheritance, whether the Temple (Jer 7:4), Bethel (Jer 48:13) or idols (Hab 2:18), and certainly not our own logic and calculations (Ps 94:11). The attitude of expectant and confident hope increasingly expresses the realization that everything in this life is provisional.

The New Testament theology of hope follows closely that of the Hebrew scriptures, while differentiating a little more clearly hope's three essential qualities: expectation, trust and patient waiting. Above all, Christ himself is our hope (Col 1:27; 1 Tm 1:1). Paul contrasts hoping to seeing (Rm 8:24-25), because everything which is visible pertains to the sphere of the fleshy.[3]

---

[3]See *Spiritual Direction*, pp. 25-27; Gerhard Kittel, ed., *Theological Dictionary of the New Testament*, Eerdmans, 1976, II, pp. 517-535.

Perhaps St. Paul's greatest contribution to the understanding of Christian hope comes through his own personal experience. Saul of Tarsus was anything but a patient man. Until his conversion, he placed absolute trust in the law and in his own abilities. Paul's encounter with Christ, however, resulted in one interior upheaval after another. After his three year sojourn in the desert, he could not sit still until he was imprisoned in Rome some thirty years later. Paul consistently speaks of his experience of hope as something tearing him up inside and wrenching out his old self. Christian hope leaves us champing at the bit with eager expectation (Rm 8:25). Christian hope is fraught with the tension of straining forward (Ph 3:13). Christian patience is a most trying virtue — just waiting, longing, yearning for God to complete doing with us what he wills. Patient hope is anything but placid, thumb-twiddling, passing the time away.

To say that Christian hope is restless is an understatement. It produces a degree of restless emptiness in us which is almost indescribable. The great mystic poets, like John of the Cross, use phrases in this vein:

Vivo sin vivir en mí,	I live without living in myself,
Y de tal manera espero,	And I have such hope,
Que muero porque no muero.[4]	That I die because I do not die.

The psalmist is no less emphatic:

> As a doe pants for running waters,
>   so my soul pines for you, my God.
> My soul thirsts for God, the God of life;
>   when shall I appear before you, Lord? (Ps 42:1-2).

> God, you are my God: I yearn for you.
> My soul thirsts for you, my flesh longs for you
>   in a land dry, weary and waterless (Ps 63:1-2).

[4]Refrain of the poem, *Vivo sin vivir.*

The restlessness of hope will not allow us to sit still. We cannot wait with arms folded. We are drawn forward from up ahead. We are prodded from within. We are pushed towards God from every side. It is impossible to rest content, for this earthly existence is not our permanent state.

The emptiness of hope is wholly positive. It is the emptiness of hunger and thirst. It seeks frantically to be filled. And by the time we reach the night of spirit, we know in every fiber of our being that only God himself is our fulfillment.

Yet there are times when even an advanced contemplative soul will try to fill up this void by more energetic engagement in some activity, by a new form of recreation, or by a fresh personal relationship. These changes may be fine in themselves and may be even relatively meaningful, but they do not and cannot fill the void hollowed out by evangelical hope. To the degree that they are sought after to serve as a diversion from this positive emptiness, they will ultimately produce nothing but frustration, dissipation and distaste. Yet, God sometimes lets us go this route in order to teach us experientially where he is not.

He for whom we long is not way out there somewhere. "Your hope is so near that he is within you."[5] So true is this that we cannot speak properly of God as the "object" of hope. God is its subject, for he is more intimate to us than we are to ourselves. Since our deification is not complete, however, Christ within us longs for completion: "I have come to cast a fire upon the earth. And how I wish it were already ablaze!" (Lk 12:49).

"The more our memory is stripped, the more hope we experience. And the more we hope, the greater is our union with God. This is so because the more we hope in God, the more we actually attain him. . . . When we are perfectly stripped of all, we shall remain in the possession of God in divine union."[6]

[5]*Canticle*, 1, 7.
[6]*Ascent*, III, 7, 2.

C. Trust and Fear

Both the Old and the New Testaments present fear, in the sense of lack of trust, as the opposite of hope in God. Paul speaks of despair only twice and this in the context of the trials of the apostolate: "The things we had to undergo in Asia were so beyond our ability to endure that we despaired of coming out of it alive" (2 Co 1:8); "We encounter difficulties on every side, but are never crushed; we are perplexed, but do not despair" (2 Co 4:8). Scholastic theology of the Middle Ages presented despair as the opposite of hope. To despair is to lose all hope, confidence or trust in something or someone. It denotes having no outlet whatsoever.

Of itself and within certain limits, fear is a healthy emotion. It is a normal reaction to certain stressful situations. The proper object of fear is the unknown. And there is nothing more unknowable than the mystery of God and of his purpose. Hebrew has two distinct words and meanings for fear: *yirah* (reverence, awe) and *pahad* (dread, terror). The first is the sense of *Proverbs* 1:7: "The fear of the Lord is the beginning of wisdom." *Yirah* is very positive and hope-filled. The Hebrews frequently used *pahad* with regard to God's judgment. This latter is not necessarily hopeless, unless of course one refuses to be changed, to be converted. In the Hebrew mentality *pahad* was often the prelude to *yirah*. If people were frightened enough of God, they might begin to reverence him, they thought. It was an exemplification of the theory that certain people, like boats, are best propelled from the rear.

Paul plays on both senses of fear, when he exhorts the Philippians (2:12-13): "Continue to work out your salvation with fear (*phobos*) and trembling (*tromos*), for it is God who works in you both to will and to act according to his good will." It is *pahad* that "perfect love drives out, because that kind of fear has to do with punishment. The one fearing in this sense has not been perfected in love" (1 Jn 4:18). *Yirah*, on the other hand, is infinitely intensified by love, faith and hope.

Thus, fear in the sense of lack of trust in God's tender love and mercy is the opposite of evangelical hope. In the night of spirit, the intense purification of hope centers around the quality and depth of our trust in God and our confidence in his providence for us. Just how real is our trust?

In letting ourselves be stripped to the bone in relation to everyone and everything, we are forced to struggle intensely with the question of trust. As I undergo the fear and emptiness of unknowing which the purgation of hope necessitates, do I honestly trust God to act in my best interest? Do I have a sense of at-homeness, peace and confidence as I journey to him in mystery? Or am I suspicious of God and filled with doubts and misgivings? Maybe I claim that I trust God, but that I have no trust in myself. This can be a way of rationalizing the fact that I really distrust his grip on me. I fear that he may let me go. Most often, we discover within ourselves mixed reactions. Basically, we do trust, yet at the same time our fear keeps us from taking the all-out plunge.

Preachers tell the story of a man falling down a precipice into the gorge below. He keeps tumbling and tumbling. About half way down he manages to grab hold of a branch sticking out of the vertical surface. As he dangles over the gorge, he cries out for dear life: "God, save me." He hears a voice: "Do you really trust me?" "God, you know I do," he prays in desperation. The voice returns: "Then, let go. . . ."

We smile at the story. But putting ourselves in that physical situation, would we have actually let go? It is a very scary thought. Transposing the analogy to the spiritual life, we have to ask: Do we truly let go?

There is a further point to the story, however. Whether in the actual physical situation or in the spiritual life, most of us do not — probably cannot — let go until we are forced to do so. Our grip has to be broken before we allow God to grip us fully. The weight of our own body, or God himself, eventually has to break that grip so that in losing ourselves, we find him (Mt 10:39).

There is yet another dimension to our fear and to what we sometimes tend to interpret as a lack of trust during this night. Often, both these feelings are in fact a reaction to the stripping away of all the trappings that have nothing to do with true growth in hope. We learn to mistrust what we should never have trusted in the first place. In dying to our unrealistic, false hopes and expectations, we are freed so as to be able to hope in all truth. Naturally, we fear the unknown element in all this detachment, and we do not quite know whom or how to trust for a while. Nonetheless, God ekes a deeper confidence out of us as we lose trust in all our peripheral ways and associations.

D. Signs of Authenticity

What signs then indicate growth in evangelical hope during the night of spirit? As usual, these signs are very paradoxical. They are basically three:

A *first* sign is this: As the gift of hope increases in us, we experience the stripping away of all our false and unrealistic hopes. Our hope in God and our longing for him are themselves transformed and purified. In this process we are gradually emptied of the attachment to everything that we possess together with all desire to possess anything. Much of what we want from God and from others simply cannot be. This discovery is painful and often very frustrating. We realize that so many of our desires are no more than idealistic pipe dreams which run counter to the stark reality of life in Christ. Even the expectations and hopes that are fulfilled — for example, reaching the top, receiving public acclaim, being recognized by our peers — ultimately leave us grappling all the more with an insatiable spiritual emptiness.

As we die to all these hopes and expectations and as God sets us more firmly upon himself in evangelical hope, we usually undergo considerable emotional upheaval. In the throes of this death to self, we normally hit bottom. What is especially frightening in this purgation is the impression that God is present at times but powerless to help us. At other times he seems absent altogether, or nonexistent. Needless to say, these surface impressions trigger feelings of intense despair and depression. Prolonged fatigue and despondency sometimes threaten to engulf us and to prevent us from praying or working as responsibly as we believe that we should. There are times when death itself would seem like a blessed relief.

If this experience arises from the night of spirit, the director will discern in the soul an emerging inner freedom, a deeper sense of detachment coupled with unflinching courage and unwavering perseverance in the face of all these trials. The presence of these qualities may appear faint at first. But they will grow more unmistakable with time. While on a behavioral level the soul may be crying out for the reality of its life in God to be different from what it presently experiences, in its inmost being the soul is becoming more accepting of God as he truly is. Despite all this emotional turmoil, we sense in such a person that growing peace and joy which the world cannot give or take away.

A *second* sign that the soul is successfully moving towards resolution of its crisis of Christian hope is this: Generally, the intensification of evangelical hope causes violent upheavals deep within the soul. These upheavals are similar to, but more forceful than, the spirit of blasphemy encountered in the night of sense. In the loss of control and possession —whether this loss consists in being no longer self-possessed or in being dispossessed of ideals and expectations — the irascible appetite tends to strike out in misguided directions. Thus, the soul is prone to be very quick-tempered and highly impatient with everyone and everything, including itself and God. Then, to compound the situation the soul becomes despondent at its own angry disposition. If these storms arise from the night of spirit, the director will see that, despite the way things appear on the surface, the soul has a profound ability to wait patiently and in eager expectation upon God. At the same time, but on different levels, the soul feels like biting someone's head off, yet intensely desires to surrender itself completely to the Lord.

A *third* sign that God is transforming and purifying his

gift of hope pertains to the nature of the emptiness which the soul endures. This emptiness is God-initiated and God-centered. It is not the result of a deliberate technique of self-emptying. This inner void cannot be produced by blocking out thoughts, images or feelings. It consists in an insatiable thirst and hunger for God in himself. It is the consequence of a profound encounter with the Lord. Hidden in all this emptiness is the *all* of God.

Chapter 17

THE LIVING FLAME AND NIGHT OF LOVE

In the end, everything is reduced to "faith, hope and love. But the greatest of these is love" (1 Co 13:13). Deep within the human heart everything is epitomized in *agape*. Three qualities characterize our love for God as we undergo the night of spirit: love unto death, the emptiness of mortal love, and our yearning for God in himself.

A. *Love unto Death*

Since the threshold of emergence, the consciousness of our personal love for God has been increasing dramatically. We have been directly aware for some time that God has been drawing us toward an ever more intimate and unconditional surrender of our whole selves to him. As we pass through the night of spirit, this awareness reaches new levels of intensity. By this time, we are living quite literally the ancient prayer of Israel: "You shall love Yahweh your God with all your heart, with all your soul and with all your strength" (Dt 6:5; Mk 12:30).

St. John of the Cross makes the following comments regarding the above invitation of the Lord: "Herein is contained all that the spiritual person must do in order to truly reach union with God by means of love. For herein we are urged to employ all our faculties, desires, activities and affections in God, so that all the ability and strength of our soul may serve him alone."[1]

In the night of spirit, however, we perceive the gaping abyss that exists between the quality of loving to which we are called and our woefully lacking, present manner of loving both God and others. John of the Cross refers to this phenomenon as "the affliction of love" in the sense that love pains us positively. Paradoxically, this awareness constitutes a positive sign of the authenticity of our love, since only true love can drive a person to desire to love more perfectly. Love makes us desire to be more loving, for love itself and our capacity to love are infinite. Furthermore, as our love becomes more refined, we develop a keen awareness of the slightest imperfection in our love. The greater our love, the more we realize our lack of it. John concludes: "The absence of this affliction of love is a sign either that the soul has no love at all or else that it has attained perfect love."[2]

Faced with this discrepancy in love, our spirit becomes anxious. We are bewildered and confused. Although we yearn to love more perfectly, we have no idea how to do so. We feel trapped in our present mode of loving and unable to transcend its innate imperfections. We wonder whether we know how to love at all.

This experience too has its positive side. Our admission that we do not know how to love, together with the sense of lostness and helplessness which this confusion entails, disposes us to let God himself teach us to love as he loves. Moreover, our sense of stagnation is only a mirage. In reality, God has been instructing us in the perfection of love for some time, without our understanding how this instruction is taking place and without our doing anything other than letting it be done.[3]

The intensity of transformation which produces the night

[1]*Ascent*, III, 16, 1. See *Night*, II, 11, 4.

[2]*Canticle*, 11, 14.

[3]See *Night*, II, 5, 1.

of spirit overpowers us with *agape*: God's own love for us. The force of his love at this time causes us to desire to love like Jesus: ". . . to the end" (Jn 13:1). "To the end" — not only in the sense of consummate perfection of love, but also in the sense of loving God to the point of complete death to self. Our whole being feels itself dying of love and longs to love unto death.

Needless to say, this burning desire encounters staunch opposition on the behavioral level. Like St. Paul, we find that "every time I want to do good, something evil rears its head. In my inmost being I dearly love God's law. But I can see that my body follows a different law, warring against the law of my mind" (Rm 7:21-23).

Paul's assessment is applicable to the night of love. We see that we know no more how to die to self than we know how to love more perfectly. We still overindulge. We are still quick-tempered and selfish. We still have bouts with vanity and lust. "Who will deliver me from this body of death?" (Rm 7:24). In fact, however, we are learning to love by simply suffering our weaknesses and helplessness, as well as by waiting patiently for God to transform us more in his time and in his way.

While we experience the luring call to love unto death, we find ourselves resisting our own longing. We resist in basically two ways: (1) Certain tendencies in us attempt to limit God's love for us. His love for us is too overwhelming and too exigent. It takes too much out of us and it costs us too much. (2) Certain elements within us try to limit our response to God's love. Consciously or unconsciously, we place conditions on our love: "provided. . . that it doesn't hurt too much. . . that I know what God is doing with me. . . that it doesn't become too dark and confusing. . . that I have something to hold on to, etc."

The critical challenge in the night of spirit is to let God's love be fully operative within us and in turn to love him without imposing any limits or conditions whatsoever. It is in this context that the sentiments expressed in Charles de Foucauld's Prayer of Abandonment take on particular significance:

Father,
I abandon myself into your hands.
Do with me what you will.
Whatever you may do, I thank you.
I am ready for all.
I accept all.
Let only your will be done in me,
    and in all your creatures.
I ask no more than this, Lord.
Into your hands I commend my soul.
I offer it to you with all the love
    of my heart.
For I love you, Lord.
And I so need to give myself to you.
    to surrender myself into your hands,
    without reserve,
    and with boundless confidence.
For you are my Father.[4]

B. *The Emptiness of Mortal Love*

Like advanced hope, love engenders an insatiable emptiness in us. It is the emptiness of being forcibly separated from our Beloved. We remain "forced" by the limitations of this mortal existence.

There is obviously a negative emptiness which we experience when we have loved wrongly or poorly. However, the positive emptiness whereof we speak is the result of having loved as well as we can under the circumstances. This emptiness occurs on both a sensory and a spiritual level.

It affects our sensory level, because our emotions cannot even begin to cope with the force of divine love within us. God's transcendent and immanent love overpowers our

[4]See Jean-Francois Six, ed., *Spiritual Autobiography of Charles de Foucauld*, Dimension Books, 1964, pp. 95-96.

capacities to feel, to imagine, to know and to will. God's love leaves these faculties arid and void in relation to their usual objects, while empowering these same faculties in a transformed and purified way. Why look at a photo of my mother, when she is in front of me? Why be concerned with concepts of God, when the whole Trinity really dwells within me? Why fuss about consolations, when I can have God himself? Why settle for a part, when I can have All?

But therein lies the other aspect of the problem. We cannot actually have All in this life. This side of the resurrection we are not yet completely spiritualized. Consequently, this emptiness attains our deepest spiritual level. The realization of the disparity between how well we do love and how infinitely more we need to love produces an indescribable spiritual emptiness which only God in himself can fill.

Thus, the phrase "emptiness of mortal love" refers not only to our love of mortal beings but also to our mode of loving God in this mortal state. John of the Cross offers this piece of hard advice: "Never seek satisfaction in what you understand about God, but only in what you do not understand of him. Never rest and delight in what you know and feel regarding God, but only in what you cannot know or feel of him."[5]

This profound spiritual emptiness which advanced love causes can be very perplexing. It gives rise to many agonizing questions and moments. "My God, my God why have you forsaken me?" (Mt 27:46; Mk 15:34). Jesus was not only quoting *Psalm* 22:1, but he was especially giving full lament to the almost unbearable emptiness of his mortal love for his Father.

Another trial of this spiritual night of love is similar to, but more vehement than, the spirit of fornication experienced in the night of sense. During the earlier night, our concupiscible appetite underwent intense purgation. Now in the night of spirit, the purification reaches even deeper to the very core of our desires to feel pleasure and to seek consolation. How the same person can love God unto

---

[5]*Canticle*, 1, 12.

death and at the same time be so strongly tempted is a typical contradiction and paradox of this night. Even this far along in transforming union we are still sinners in a very existential sense. These storms arise at this time from two basic sources: (1) Lust, vanity, pleasure-seeking continue to exist within us at this stage of development. (2) Our concupiscible appetite itself lashes out frantically in any direction that might afford some relief from this seemingly interminable aridity.

Three signs indicate progress through the spiritual night of love: single-heartedness, selflessness and equanimity.

(1) God uses the condition of emptiness which this night generates as a means of directing us more lovingly and singleheartedly to him alone. For in this barrenness we can love nothing, rest in nothing or find relief in nothing apart from him. Thus, in the night of spirit, "the soul who truly loves God is recognized by this sign: It is content with nothing less than God himself."[6] It is "clean of heart" (Mt 5:8).

(2) The night of spirit uproots our egocentrism, setting us more firmly on the road of selflessness and Other-centeredness. "If the soul loves God, its heart will not be turned in upon itself or preoccupied with its own pleasure and glory. Rather, it will be intent upon giving honor and glory to God and upon giving him pleasure. To the degree that we are centered on self, we love God that much less."[7]

(3) A third sign that we are centered in love upon God alone is the spirit of equanimity with which we bear all things — joys and sorrows, pleasure and suffering — for the sake of Christ. "True love receives everything that comes from its Beloved. Adversity, prosperity, chastisement: all are endured with the same equanimity and sense of detachment. This attitude becomes our joy and our delight."[8]

---

[6] *Canticle*, 1, 14.

[7] *Canticle*, 9, 5.

[8] *Canticle*, 11, 10.

C. Yearning for God in Himself

The intensity of the living flame of love in the night of spirit is such that it enkindles in us vehement and insatiable yearnings for God in himself. He is now our Beloved in the fullest sense of the word. This longing arises from the fact that, although we are more consciously and more directly seeking God in love than ever before, we are also made more acutely aware that our union with him is still incomplete. Until our union in love is brought to its perfection, "we remain like an empty vessel waiting to be filled, like a hungry person starving for food, like a sick man or woman pining for health, like someone suspended in mid air without any support. Such is the heart of those who have truly fallen in love: It is empty, hungry, solitary, mortally wounded, love-sick, up in the air."[9]

Of all the characteristics of love in the night of spirit, it is this yearning for God which John of the Cross emphasizes most. This longing arises from the inner dynamics of love. By its very nature, love demands the full presence and undivided attention of its Beloved.

Stanzas 8-9 of the poem *The Spiritual Canticle* describe the impatient pleading of the soul with God as it longs for him to bring its wound of love to completion. First, the soul addresses its own situation:

> How do you go on, oh life of mine,
> Not living where you live?
> You are brought near death
> By the piercings of love
> Which your Beloved has brought forth from within you.

Then, the soul addresses its Beloved:

> Since you have sorely wounded this heart,
> Why don't you heal it?

[9]*Canticle,* 9, 6.

And since you have stolen it from me,
Why do you leave it languishing?
Why don't you take fully to yourself what you have
stolen?

The soul finds that, because of the loving surrender of itself to God, it no longer belongs to itself. And yet, because it has not died and been resurrected, it does not belong totally to God either. This condition of having gone out from itself and not yet being completely transformed in God translates into an anguished yearning, hungering, thirsting for God in himself. Thus, love has within itself a dynamic thrust towards ever deeper and more perfect love of God and of all creation in him. The only cure for the wound of love in this life is ever greater love in the next. The more we love, the more we are enflamed to love "to the end" (Jn 13:1). Mortally wounded by love, we cannot rest until we can love God as perfectly as he loves us and with his own love.

This languishing in love is experienced in every facet of our personality: emotions, nervous system, psyche, etc. Moreover, it continues even when we do not feel it operative or directly advert to its presence within us.

In the beginning of the night of spirit, our yearnings in love had manifested themselves primarily through a kind of spiritual anxiety. Anguished thoughts arose which made us wonder whether we had lost God or whether he had abandoned us. As we progress through this night, however, those anxious questions dissipate. What remains is the subtle, but unmistakable, experience of the indwelling Trinity. God knowing himself in us is faith. God longing in us to recapitulate all creation in Christ is hope. The Father and the Son spirating the Holy Spirit in us is love.

FINAL THRESHOLDS

Chapter 18

SPIRITUAL ESPOUSAL

I will espouse you to myself forever.
I will espouse you with integrity and justice,
    with tenderness and love.
I will espouse you to myself with fidelity.
Then you shall experience me as Yahweh (Ho 2:21-22).

In Western thought, to espouse or to betroth means to promise to marry or to give in marriage. The Hebrew *aras* denotes being at the point of full-fledged marriage and in some cases actually being married, but without as yet necessarily living together. Thus, Mary was "espoused" to Joseph (*emnesteumenen*) at the time of the annunciation (Lk 1:27). Yet, she is referred to again as "his espoused one" at the nativity (Lk 2:5). Luke uses the same word in reference to both before and after they came to live together. Matthew, on the other hand, speaks of Mary as "being espoused" to Joseph when he discovered her pregnant (Mt 1:18), but refers to her as Joseph's "wife" (*gynaika*) during and after his ordeal (Mt 1:20, 24-25). Whatever the exact biblical meanings of the words in question, the terms "espousal" and "marriage" do not correspond exactly — either socially or juridically —to what we call today "engagement" and "marriage."

Be that as it may, our spiritual espousal constitutes a further critical threshold in the process of divinization. It is, moreover, the immediate prelude to spiritual marriage.

Throughout the previous ten chapters of this book we

have been considering the maze of interrelated dimensions which make up our emergence through creation with Christ. Many persons spend virtually their entire lives creeping through the stage of immersion. Emergence for them occurs right at the end or in death itself. Many others, however, are drawn into emergence relatively soon, and they spend most of their adult lives passing through its manifold dimensions. This side of death, comparatively few persons actually reach the threshold of spiritual espousal and a fortiori spiritual marriage. Yet, experience has proven that many more do reach these latter thresholds than is generally assumed.

Most authors on the interior life speak of spiritual espousal in the context of mystical union, and rightly so. However, by virtue of the universal call to holiness we are all called to mystical union and mystic prayer.[1] We are all destined for total loving surrender to God. The adjective "mystical" or "mystic" refers to God's direct and immediate activity within the soul, coupled with the soul's awareness of that fact. Thus, "mystical" is basically synonymous with "contemplative." Generally though, the word "mystical" is reserved to designate the more advanced stages of the contemplative movement. Moreover, at the earlier stages of contemplation we are not usually aware of God's direct activity within us.

St. John of the Cross' final line of *The Summa of Perfection* — "remaining loving our Beloved" — describes not only the quintessence of eternal life, but also the quintessence of this mortal life as well. The final human act for each of us is eminently a contemplative act of total, loving abandonment to God. Hence, this act is also eminently mystical. It is not all that uncommon to encounter authentic mystical union — spiritual espousal — in the case of the terminally ill. Some hospices may contain more real contemplatives and mystics than do some monasteries. We just do not recognize these persons as such, nor do they recognize themselves in that light. The emotional and psychological resignation which terminates months of denial, anger, bar-

---

[1]See *Contemplation*, pp. 13-20.

gaining, etc. is frequently the sensory effect of full-blown mystic prayer.

A. *Betrothed by God to Christ*

In passing through the night of spirit, we eventually arrive at a point where God's love for us has reached such a pitch of intensity that we cross a further critical threshold. The most apt analogy to describe the grace in question is that of divine betrothal. John of the Cross puts it this way: "After much spiritual exercising, God places us in this exalted state and union of love. This state is called spiritual espousal with the Word, the Son of God."[2]

The initiative in this threshold is entirely God's. We cannot of ourselves even desire this degree of union. God's love for us directly produces it from within us. Moreover, this espousal occurs only after we have undergone a lifetime of transformation and purgation. This divine preparation is both qualitatively intensive and quantitatively extensive in that it attains every facet of our being and of our daily lives. The living flame of divine love reaches such a point of actuality that we are enflamed with love for God. We not only love him, but specifically we are *in* love with him. We are being consumed in love.

We are in love with Father, Son and Spirit. In a certain sense, it is true to say that the élan of mystical union begins with the threshold of emergence. For there, God himself starts taking *direct* charge of our life and destiny. This same élan has now reached a point of radical and critical intensity. And while its focus is being in love with Father, Son and Spirit, the person of the eternal Word made flesh is especially accentuated. At the very apex of mystical union in this life, we enter into a transformed relationship in love specifically with the person of Christ Jesus.

This truth has further implications. The Church and the sacraments take on a new and transformed significance. By

---

[2]*Canticle*, 14, 2: "...*desposorio espiritual con el Verbo Hijo de Dios*."

this stage of interior development, we have become emancipated pilgrims. We have passed beyond the externals of the institutional Church and of its liturgical rites to penetrate the very core of the mystery which they are supposed to represent. Thus, our participation in the Church and our celebration of the sacraments are more meaningful than before. It is the rapport of mature adults with their parents. The bond of love and the dynamics of spiritual communion are more vibrant than ever.

Although the essence of spiritual espousal remains union with God in love, each person experiences this grace in a unique way. "It must not be thought that God communicates with everyone who reaches this stage . . . in exactly the same manner or in the same measure. To some he gives more, to others less; to some in one way, to others in another, although each one may be enjoying this state of spiritual espousal."[3]

B. Mystical Graces

The mystical grace of all is direct and immediate communion with Father, Son and Spirit to an ever greater degree, coupled with increased personal awareness of this loving communion. Any other gift of the mystical order is purely accessory, and pertains to the diverse manners in which God deals with different people. For many, the grace of spiritual espousal transpires in a protracted state of *nada* (nothingness). There is no particular feeling or manifestation on any perceptible level. Yet, these souls intuit in the darkness of their faith the loving bond which God is deepening. For others, the grace of spiritual espousal is accompanied by certain mystical favors such as locutions, visions, illuminations, touches, etc. Some of these can be very painful both physically and emotionally.

God rarely bestows these gifts in any extraordinary way. By this we mean that any soul actually aware of its intensifying communion with God is also going to be aware of subtle

[3] *Canticle*, 14, 2.

inspirations coming directly from God out of this communion. We "see" things we never saw before (Mt 13:16-17; Act
2:17). We understand truths we never appreciated before. If
we truly listen to God, we are bound to "hear" a few things
once in a while. If we love so intensely that we are dying
because we cannot yet die, we will surely "feel" a few things
as well. All of this is normal and "ordinary" not only during
spiritual espousal, but also intermittently throughout our
whole spiritual genesis. God delights in transforming us in
ordinary ways. He takes pleasure in communing with us in a
simple, down-to-earth manner. When he deals with us in an
extraordinary fashion, it is because he wants to for some
particular reason. That reason is usually known only to
himself.

For the most part, these extraordinary gifts pertain to the
charismata, since they are for our personal benefit and
sometimes also for that of others. These gifts are not strictly
what the scholastics called "sanctifying grace" (*gratia gra-
tum faciens*). They approximate rather what the schoolmen
termed "free gifts" (*gratiae gratis datae*). These graces need
not presuppose spiritual espousal at all. In fact, they can
occur anywhere along life's interior journey. Moreover, the
personal holiness of the individual receiving these extraordinary gifts is neither confirmed nor denied on the basis of
these gifts. We are neither better nor worse off, per se, for
having them or for not having them.

Apostleship is one of the *charismata*. But we can legitimately suspect a great difference in holiness between St.
Peter and Judas. Prophecy is also a charism. But there exists
wide divergence between the faith of St. Paul and that of
Caiaphas (Jn 11:49-52). People from all over the world went
out of their way to see the stigmatic Padre Pio. But who is to
say that he was in any deeper communion with God than a
poor peasant left to rot by a death squad in El Salvador?

What should be our attitude towards these gifts — ordinary or extraordinary — if and when they occur? They are
given by God for our own personal benefit and sometimes
also for that of others. If God wants us to do something
particular in relation to these gifts, he will surely inspire us

to do exactly what he wants. In the absence of such inspiration, he wants us to do nothing other than simply receive the gift and let him do whatever he wills with it. We must never desire such gifts or become attached to them. When they do occur, we ought to let them come and go as God wills.

God does not even want recipients to be concerned with discerning the authenticity of their experience. "God does not expect them to undertake this labor, nor does he wish that sincere and simple souls should be exposed to the danger and inner conflicts which such a discernment might entail. They have the incomparable gift of faith. And it is by faith that they are always to journey forward."[4]

Unless there are unusual circumstances connected with these gifts — for example: notoriety, excessive turmoil, a particular message, etc. — the spiritual directors of these recipients should pay as little attention as possible to these events. Both the director and the recipient need to focus their respective attention on faith — dark faith. If these gifts are authentic, they flow from faith and lead to deeper faith in God. If they are partly or purely imaginary, God will use what he wants out of the situation and let the rest fall away. If they are a hoax, then we are dealing with deliberate deception.

When these gifts are of a public nature, competent ecclesiastical authorities have to be brought into the picture. Their principal responsibility, however, is to rule out fraud. If the signs point towards possible authenticity, they too should receive whatever God wills to bestow through the gift, downplay as much as possible the extraordinariness of the situation, and continue to journey to God in dark faith, encouraging all others to do the same.

C. God and the Soul in Love with Each Other

Love has reasons that reason can never know. Whatever gifts God may give, the greatest gift of all is his infinite love

[4]*Ascent*, II, 16, 14.

for each individual. For in loving us, he gives us himself and makes us capable of loving him with his own love.

The most striking characteristic of the soul at the threshold of spiritual espousal is the quality of its love for God. We do not just love him. We are in love with God — more intimately, more passionately, more wholeheartedly than before. The espoused soul in love with God abides in a stance of inner fascination and wonder before the mystery of the indwelling Trinity. God has so captivated and enchanted us that we are plunged ever deeper into the mystery of the divine persons. We are caught up in God, dazzled by his beauty and absorbed in his infinite love. So enraptured are we by Father, Son and Spirit that we experience an irresistible urge to go out of ourselves so as to live totally in God. We are ecstatic to the point that with all our being we long for God to become fully our All.

In spiritual espousal, although we realize that we are already deeply in union with God, we still remain acutely aware that our communion with him is not yet complete. In fact, the very depth of the experience of union which characterizes spiritual betrothal increases our awareness of an indescribable lack within ourselves. We taste our insatiability more profoundly than ever. Love continues to draw us to greater love. The experience of union with God in spiritual espousal fires us with an unquenchable thirst and a consuming desire for more perfect communion in love.

The soul espoused to the divine Word yearns to give itself in total, irrevocable, loving abandonment. All that we are, all that we have and all that we are destined to become, we seek to surrender to God. In pining to give ourselves to God in complete, loving abandonment, we crave equally to receive God in himself. To reach this goal, we resolutely risk being unconditionally open and vulnerable. We are committed to courageously follow wherever the Spirit leads, no matter how dark or hazardous the way.

Besides experiencing itself in love with God, the espoused soul is also conscious that God is in love with it. This realization humbles us as no humiliation can. This realization also excites and invigorates us, making us rejoice in

God as never before (Lk 1:46-47). In our divine espousal we experience that God has truly promised himself to us. Moreover, he too longs that our union in love be brought to perfection. If we lovingly desire God, he desires us infinitely more. God yearns to surrender himself totally to us and to make us completely his own. Nonetheless, he must still further prepare us to receive the fullness of this mutual exchange of love.

In spiritual espousal, love intensifies the movement of both the Beloved and the soul towards each other. God is consuming us ever more fully from within our inmost being, and we are being drawn ever more resolutely into him. This intensification flows from the force of God's infinite love for us and from our insatiable loving quest for God in himself.

We experience undeniably in spiritual espousal that God is truly becoming all in all (1 Co 15:28), as well as all in us. We experience this welling up of the Trinity not only directly within ourselves but also in and through everything created. All creation is filled with the "silent music" and "sounding solitude" of our Lord.[5] As a consequence of its profoundly interior communion with Father, Son and Spirit, the espoused soul has received a transformed way of looking at the world. It sees beyond appearances to Christ recapitulating all in himself (Col 1:15-20) at the heart of matter.

Furthermore, our interior loving communion with the Trinity is the integrating factor in our whole life, whether we are alone or with others, at work or at play, in activity or in leisure. The encounter with God in spiritual espousal effects in us a deeper encounter with the entirety of creation. We experience that our interpersonal union with God in love is the basis of our solidarity with all creatures. Spiritual betrothal awakens in us a heightened sense of cosmic oneness in God. For it is in him that absolutely everything lives and moves and has its being (Ac 17:28). We cannot be in true communion with the Trinity without simultaneously being in communion with the entire cosmos.

[5]*Canticle*, stanza 15.

D. The Tranquil Night

Spiritual espousal marks a shift of emphasis in terms of our involvement with creatures. Since the threshold of emergence, the most striking aspect of our overall experience with creation has been one of detachment. We have been acutely aware of aridity with regard to everything created. We have felt the pain of having to gradually and systematically let go — at least interiorly — all those persons and things to which we were attached. Detachment is still an essential part of the stage of spiritual espousal. However, the quality of our life in God is such that we are now more focused on our freedom to enjoy and to take pleasure in creatures without clinging to them. Having left all things according to affection and will,[6] we now possess the capacity to enjoy all things in God. This new attitude is one of the positive fruits of the night of spirit. "Even though this blessed night darkens the spirit, it does so only to impart light in all things. And even though it humbles us and reveals our miseries, it does so only to exalt us. And even though it impoverishes us and empties us of all possessions and natural affections, it does so only that we may reach forward divinely to the enjoyment of all earthly and heavenly things, while maintaining a general freedom of spirit with regard to them all."[7]

The spiritual espousal also marks a change in our perception of ourselves. Up to this point in the night, we had for the most part undergone the overpowering experience of our wretchedness. In divine betrothal, God continues to reveal to us the depths of our inner poverty. Yet, he also increasingly reveals to us the spiritual riches with which he has endowed us. The interior disposition of the spiritually espoused person is like that of Mary: "My soul praises the Lord and my spirit rejoices in God my Savior, because he has looked upon his servant in her poverty" (Lk 1:46-48).

Moreover, the espoused soul becomes more conscious of

---

[6]See *Canticle*, 1, 6; *Ascent*, 1, 3, 1-4; *Receptivity*, pp. 18-23, 41-49.
[7]*Night*, II, 9, 1.

the mystery of its personal identity in God. Paradoxically, the more that we abandon ourselves to God in loving union, the more we come into the fullness of our own unique personhood. "Whoever wants to save his/her life will lose it, but the one who loses his/her life for my sake will find it" (Mt 16:25). True union in love always differentiates. The more perfect the communion, the more accomplished the differentiation.

Besides coming to know ourselves and creation in a transformed way, we receive in spiritual espousal a more intensified loving knowledge of God. This is a general, loving, obscure, experiential knowledge which transcends particular concepts and images. It is delicate, subtle, ineffable, simple and elusive. "It is like the air which escapes when one tries to grasp it."[8] This is a sapiential experience of what most uniquely constitutes God as God. It is knowing him more deeply by unknowing.

The night of spirit does not cease when God espouses us to his eternal Word. Although he has betrothed us to himself, we are still not yet totally transformed in him or completely purified of every vestige of selfishness. Nonetheless, while the night continues, with the onset of spiritual espousal it enters into a new phase. John of the Cross compares it to "the tranquil night at the time of the approaching dawn."[9]

As the soul espoused to Christ Jesus continues its journey to the Father, the purifying activity of God will at times be more wrenching and painful than before. For there still remain deep-seated imperfections which God must purge. Yet, even in undergoing these trials, we henceforth experience the night as predominately peaceful and tranquil. "In this spiritual sleep which the soul enjoys reposing upon the bosom of its Beloved, it experiences all the tranquillity and restfulness of this peaceful night. . . . This calm and quietness in God is not dark in the same way as the earlier stages

---

[8] *Night*, I, 9, 6.

[9] *Canticle*, stanza 15: *la noche sosegada en par de los levantes de la aurora.* *Sosegada* means calm, quiet, restful, composed, tranquil.

of the night. . . . Rather, it is tranquillity and peacefulness in divine light and in new knowledge of God. Therein our spirit is most gently quiet now that it has been raised up to divine light."[10]

This tranquillity arises from the superabundance of the peace of Christ welling up within us — that peace which the world cannot give and cannot take away (Jn 14:27). In spiritual espousal, God besieges and inundates us so forcibly that it seems like "all the rivers of the world are flooding in upon us."[11] Yet, these resounding rivers are inundations of peace, love and tenderness.

[10]*Canticle*, 15, 22-23.
[11]*Canticle*, 14, 9.

Chapter 19

SPIRITUAL MARRIAGE

Throughout the stage of spiritual espousal, we continue to grow in the knowledge and perfection of love: love of God, love of ourselves, love of all creation. Contemplating ever more deeply the indwelling Trinity we are drawn "from glory to glory" (2 Co 3:18). Eventually, God bestows on us the last "glory" short of death: spiritual marriage.

We do not reach this threshold "without first passing through the stage of spiritual espousal; that is, through the faithful and mutual love of betrothed persons. Only after we have been espoused for some time to the Word incarnate —in a love made more perfect and tender — does God call us forth to consummate this most blessed state of marriage with himself (*a consumar . . . el matrimonio consigo*). The union between the two natures and the sharing of the divine with the human is such that, even though the one remains truly God and the other truly human, both appear to be God (*cada una parece Dios*)."[1]

A. Consummate Love

This deeper participation in the life of God effects an even more radical intensification of the qualities characteristic of spiritual espousal. We are more deeply in love with God.

[1]*Canticle*, 22, 5 (in the Spanish B.A.C. edition). English translations differ with regard to paragraph enumerations.

Our loving knowledge of him has increased. The night has become more serene and peaceful. Our awareness of the experience of God becoming all in all has sharpened. We are capable of enjoying everything created with still greater freedom of spirit. We perceive more clearly the graces and gifts which our Beloved bestows on us in our poverty.

Yet, "spiritual marriage is incomparably greater than spiritual espousal, because it is a total transformation in the Beloved wherein each surrenders the entire possession of self to the other with a certain consummation of the union of love. The soul is divinized and becomes God by participation (*está el ama hecha divina y Dios por participación*)." [2]

The mystery underlying spiritual marriage is this: God desires to surrender himself in love to us as fully as possible in this life, and God calls us to surrender ourselves in love to him insofar as this is possible in this life. In freely responding to this call, we are divinized and become God by participation. All this happens "insofar as it is possible in this life." Thus, prior to death spiritual marriage is the final critical threshold in our spiritual genesis. Beyond the threshold of spiritual marriage as such there continues what might be called the rest of our spiritual married life. In this stage the mutual love of God and the soul grows stronger and more perfect. The soul continues to become more divinized and to appear more God-like.

Communing in love with God in spiritual marriage, we are led to the inescapable experience and the profound intuition of each of the divine persons. We encounter the Father, so infinitely loving, gracious, caring, compassionate, forgiving and accepting. We encounter the Son, drawing us to the Father and giving himself up for each of us. We encounter the Holy Spirit who in secret and in mystery unites us to the Father and the Son. "Oh, the depths of the riches, the wisdom and the knowledge of God! How inscrutable his judgments, how mysterious his ways!" (Rm 11:33).

The depths from which God gives himself to us in spiri-

---

[2] *Canticle*, 22, 3.

tual marriage are such that they cause further radical transformation and purgation of our whole being. Not only do we
undergo intense purification immediately preceding spiritual marriage, but particularly in crossing the threshold
itself we experience a new intensity of death to self. Yet, in
and through this dying our true self emerges more fully
formed in the likeness of Christ. Stanzas 20-22 of *The
Spiritual Canticle* describe in symbolic form some of the
paradoxes of this mystery. The bridegroom, Christ, insists:

> Swift-winged birds,
> Lions, stags, leaping does,
> Mountains, valleys, river banks,
> Water, gales, ardent fires,
> And watchful terrors of night:
>
> By the soothing lyres
> And the sirens' song, I conjure you
> Cease your onslaught,
> And do not touch the wall
> So that the Bride may sleep in deeper peace.
>
> The Bride has entered
> The delightful garden of her desire
> And she rests to her heart's content,
> Laying her neck
> Upon the gentle arms of her Beloved.

B. *Todo, Todo, Todo — Nada, Nada, Nada*

The transforming aspect of God's indwelling at spiritual
marriage is such that now the Son, together with the Father
and the Spirit, dwells within the soul as fully as possible in
this life. The exclamation of St. Paul has reached its mortal
apex: "I live now, no longer I, but Christ lives in me" (Ga
2:20). The purifying aspect of God's love is such that it calls
forth the most complete surrender of oneself that is possible
this side of death. We give our all to God. We do so to such
an extent and depth that henceforth we belong entirely to

him alone. Finally, we love God with all our heart, with all our soul, with all our strength (Dt 6:4-5; Mk 12:30). He is our All. Until we reach our personal death, there still remain more dying and transforming. These final throes, however, consist in putting the finishing touches on a masterpiece which is virtually completed.

One may ask: Concretely, what is the soul's experience after this mutual surrender? Can there possibly by anything left? Yes, something still remains: *nada.* That is, aridity, emptiness, desert. In his *Sketch of the Ascent of Mount Carmel,* John of the Cross describes the way to the top of the mountain in this manner: "*Nada, nada, nada,* and even on the Mount *nada.*" Then John adds: "Hereon out, there is no road because for the just man/woman there is no law." There is only the freedom of the children of God, in love with him. Paradoxically, this *nada* is also *todo* (all). *Nada* is completely and continuously permeated with the presence of Father, Son and Spirit whom we encounter with indescribable faith, hope and love. Thus, the soul's experience is that of *nada* and *todo* at the same time.

As profound as the union between God and the soul is throughout spiritual marriage, this union is not yet perfect in the full sense. "In this life union with God cannot be literally perfect, even though it is beyond all words and thought."[3] We still yearn and long for God in this final stage. For we lack the perfect enjoyment of God in himself which comes only in eternal life.

Whatever we have experienced of life in God thus far, infinitely more is still to come. "No eye has seen, no ear has heard, it has not even so much as entered into the heart of anyone what God has prepared for those who love him" (1 Co 2:9). Precisely what the fullness of transforming union consists in remains hidden to us this side of the resurrection. "What we shall be in the future has not yet been revealed. All we know is that when he is revealed we shall be like him because we shall see him as he is" (1 Jn 3:2).

---

[3] *Canticle,* 22, 5.

C. The Serene Night

Because of the depth of its transforming union in love with God, the soul who has received the grace of spiritual marriage has a premonition of the resurrection. Through the experience of its transformation in God, it glimpses something of the fullness which lies immediately up ahead. John of the Cross describes symbolically this intuition of eternal life in stanzas 36-40 of *The Spiritual Canticle*. We cite some of the more poignant lines:

> Let us rejoice together, Beloved,
> And let us go forth.... (36)

> To the lofty caverns of rock
> Which are so well concealed,
> There we shall enter
> And taste new wine.... (37)

> There you will show me
> What my soul has been seeking.
> Then and there, you, who are my Life,
> Will give me completely
> What you gave me on that other day: (38)

> The breathing of air,
> The song of the sweet nightingale,
> The forest adorned with beauty,
> All during the serene night
> With a flame that is consuming and painless. (39)

The Holy Spirit, the breath of love of the Father and the Son, empowers the transformed soul to breathe in God. The Spirit thus unites God and the soul in participant transformation ("the breathing of air"). Moved by the Spirit, the soul encounters the unfathomable mystery of Christ in all his fullness ("the song of the sweet nightingale"). In discovering all creation rooted and grounded in God ("the forest adorned with beauty"), the soul finds itself, in God, in communion with all. This transpires in beatific and clear contemplation of God ("the serene night"). Contemplation itself is then simply a living flame of love which is eternally "consuming and painless," transforming and delightful, ever filling us with the utter fullness of God himself.

The sharpness of this intuition of eternal life is an aspect of spiritual marriage which distinguishes it from spiritual espousal. Because of the deeper union in love with God, the goal of the journey is imminent. It is at hand. So attracted and drawn are we by the fullness of God up ahead that arrival at the goal is in truth "the only thing necessary" (Lk 10:42). Our whole self, with all our energies, desires and affections, is straining forward towards eternal life in the Trinity (Ph 3:10-15). So near are we to eternity that we feel the fulfillment of our longing just slightly eluding our grasp. So profoundly have we already plumbed the height and the depth, the breadth and the length of God's love and so keen is our intuition of the resurrection that only a thin, transparent veil now separates us from fully encountering God in himself.

Experientially, the grace of spiritual marriage makes us realize that our life in this world has run its course. In spiritual espousal, on the other hand, while we yearn for perfect union with God, we are aware that a comparatively lengthy time in this life is still required in order for God to accomplish the necessary transformation and purification. In spiritual marriage, there persists a deep peace, gratitude and joy for all that we have received. There is a readiness for and an eager anticipation of death. The following is the prayer of the soul at this final stage of spiritual maturity:

> Oh, living flame of love,
> Which so tenderly wounds my soul in its deepest core!
> Since you are practically within my grasp,
> Finish me off now, if you will.
> Break through this transparent veil
>   which separates us.[4]

[4] *Flame*, stanza 1.

The author of 2 Timothy 4:6-7, reflecting upon his own spiritual journey, expresses sentiments akin to those of St. John of the Cross: "I am already being poured out like a libation. The time has come for me to move on. I have fought the good fight. I have run the race to the finish. I have kept the faith. All that remains is to receive the crown of holiness reserved for me, which the Lord will bestow on that day."

This yearning for death springs not from disillusionment with life, but rather from the call to imbibe life at its source. Moreover, this depth of spiritual maturity, with its premonition of impending death, need not necessarily coincide with old age. It is entirely a question of the mystery of God's transforming and purifying love operative within us. For some persons, God accomplishes much in a short time. "Length of days is not what makes age honorable. Nor are many years the true measure of life.... Being made perfect in a short time, one can achieve long life. For thus it has pleased the Lord" (Ws 4:8-14).

Nonetheless, until God's time arrives for us to enter the fullness of transforming union through our personal death, we can only wait in peaceful and patient expectation. We hear our Beloved saying: "Behold, I am coming quickly!" (Rv 22:7). Our interior attitude is: "Amen. Come, Lord Jesus" (Rv 22:20).

In waiting for our Beloved, however, we experience that we must attend to unfinished business. We have not yet completed all to which the Father has commissioned us. While we eagerly await our return with Jesus to the Father, we are aware of a renewed sense of mission. We are impelled to go forth and minister in a new spirit and sometimes in a new way. We love and care for creation as never before. Now that we are so deeply transformed in Christ, the prophetic dimension of our vocation reaches its apex. We readily perceive and proclaim the Lord's presence at the heart of the world and within the heart of each person. We collaborate with God to our utmost in the mystery of Christ recapitulating all in himself.

St. John of the Cross refers to this final stage of the night as "serene": *noche serena.*[5] The Spanish *serena (o)* can mean several things, and John plays on them all. As an adjective, it denotes something serene, calm, unruffled, quiet. As a noun, it can mean the early morning dew or the patchy fog which dots the landscape just at sunrise. Specifically as a masculine noun, it can refer to the final night-watch or to the last night watchman. Specifically as a feminine noun, it can mean serenade.

As the two arms of God's all-embracing love tighten in spiritual marriage, they come so close together that the purgative aspect is hardly distinguishable from the transforming thrust. Night and day practically coincide in a single act of consuming love.

Thus, the final stage of the dark night of our soul is serene and calm, quiet and peace-filled. We can already see the light, even though dimly as through a patch of fog. Morning has broken, day has begun. Drops of the morning dew are distinguishable upon the grass. They are starting to sparkle. Love's serenade has reached its peak. It is time for the night watchman to take his rest. Such is the *noche serena* of our soul.

D. *Discernment Related to Spiritual Espousal and Marriage*

Very rarely, if at all, are spiritual directors called upon to direct persons who have passed beyond the thresholds of spiritual espousal or spiritual marriage. There are two basic reasons for this fact. *First*, this side of the resurrection only few people enter these depths of union with God in a way that is perceptible to others. *Second*, those who do reach these depths of union before death do not usually need a spiritual director on a regular basis. God is so present within them that these persons possess sufficient wisdom to discern on their own.

However, while they may be called upon only rarely to assist such souls, spiritual directors do encounter certain

[5] *Canticle*, stanza 39.

persons who falsely claim to be in these stages of union. What signs therefore indicate to a director authentic spiritual espousal or marriage?

These thresholds are so spiritual, subtle and mysterious that it is difficult to formulate specific positive principles of discernment other than those broad lineaments of the experience which we have described in these last two chapters. In addition to those indications, we present six counterindications or negative signs regarding the mystery at hand. If it remains extremely difficult to affirm positively that someone is experiencing spiritual espousal or marriage, at least we can be fairly sure when they are not. Moreover, a person actually in these stages of mystical union needs no external reassurance. The internal evidence of the experience itself is too unmistakable. The presence of some or all the following signs rule out the authenticity of either of these thresholds.

(1) A person may believe s/he has reached spiritual espousal or spiritual marriage simply from misunderstanding the terminology. One just entering upon the threshold of immersion may mistake his/her first loving encounters with the persons of the Trinity for the grace of espousal. Another may mistake the beginnings of contemplation — when we necessarily become aware of Father, Son and Spirit actually dwelling within us — for spiritual marriage.

(2) A second area of negative indication is the lack of an integrating prayer life.[6] That is, the directee's prayer is not a prime factor integrating all the other dimensions of his/her life. Instead of a basic harmony between such apparent opposites as solitude and community, contemplation and ministry, receptivity and activity, the directee experiences head-on clash, excessive tension or outright dichotomy.

S/he may demand, for example, to have more external solitude, insisting that ministry is interfering with interior development.[7] Or the directee may perceive his/her relationship with God as something quite separate from daily life. Again, s/he may fall into a passivist attitude, always waiting for God to provide for every need, without exerting

---

[6]See *Contemplation*, pp. 125-140.
[7]See *Contemplation*, pp. 97-109.

the creativity, initiative or effort necessary to cooperate with grace.

(3) Lack of the interior development which precedes spiritual espousal or spiritual marriage is a sure sign that the soul has not reached these depths of mystical union. The process of deification unfolds progressively. God is not bound to work in any particular way, of course. He can, if he chooses, accomplish very quickly any or all stages of spiritual genesis. But everyone passes through the whole gamut of critical thresholds, if not extensively in time, at least intensively at the same time. No one jumps over any critical threshold. One does not jump from the night of sense to the tranquil night without somehow passing through the purgation of spirit.

Indications that a person has not passed through the thresholds presupposed by spiritual espousal and spiritual marriage include the following: (a) The soul's faith, hope and love have not yet been radically purified and perfected. (b) The other virtues (for instance: gentleness, patience, temperance, equanimity) are insufficiently developed. (c) The soul has little or no personal experience of the salvific effects of suffering in its life history.

(4) Attachment to any form of sensory experience of God is a further counterindication.

For instance, the directee may be consciously or unconsciously seeking emotional highs, such as strong feelings of love, intimacy or consolation. If these things do not happen spontaneously, the directee tries to induce them. Equating spiritual espousal or spiritual marriage with such extraordinary phenomena as visions, locutions, ecstacy, etc., the directee may convince him/herself that these things are occurring. Or, if something along this line does happen, s/he makes more of it than God intends.

In the latter instance, while the directee claims to be espoused to God, careful discernment reveals that s/he has no idea — either experientially or intellectually — what true contemplation really is.

Frequently, inexperienced directors flounder when their directees claim to have mystical experiences. Sometimes such directors are naively impressed. This naiveté encourages such persons to dwell unduly on these phenomena, assuming of course that they are authentic in the first place. At other times, these directors sense something amiss, but lack the knowledge or the self-confidence to confront the issue, especially when directees arrogantly insist on the authenticity of their experiences.

(5) The soul's manner of describing what it believes to be spiritual espousal or spiritual marriage is very revealing. A description which is exact, clear-cut and detailed is a negative sign, since the mysterious and ineffable nature of these thresholds transcends all logic and precision. Propensities to exaggeration and sentimentality are also counterindicative. The director should be wary if the directee tries to prove the authenticity of his/her experience with textbook descriptions and arguments.

A further negative sign in this area is the tendency of a directee to blabber indiscriminately about his/her experiences. This indiscretion usually arises from a need for attention and is completely contrary to the inner solitude which an espoused soul spontaneously seeks to maintain. "Be silent concerning what God may have given you, and remember that saying of the spouse: 'My secret is for myself' [Is 24:16]."[8]

Pious affectation in bodily gestures, facial expressions or words when one is praying in the presence of others raises serious questions. Is the soul seeking to shine in the eyes of others by appearing holy or prayerful? Is this behavior arising from pride? Is this a person of low self-esteem who is seeking approval and affirmation by means of this display?

(6) Complacency, often combined with a certain smugness, is a further negative sign. In this instance, the soul may exhibit an attitude of "having arrived." Thinking that it has reached the peak of mystical union, the soul in effect ceases to search for God. It does not allow itself to be challenged. It refuses guidance from its director, superior, community or family.

---

[8]John of the Cross, *Dichos de luz y amor*, n. 152. Is 24:16 is quoted here according to the Vulgate.

Conclusion: Personal Death

Despite all superficial observations to the contrary, every human person is a masterpiece of God. He himself creates the masterpiece over an entire lifetime. Physically, most of us peak relatively early — between twenty and thirty years of age. After that, it is downhill, for some more rapidly than for others. Spiritually, our life is a crescendo that keeps building more and more intensely. It reaches its peak when physically we are most depleted. "Although exteriorly we are fading away, interiorly we are being transformed day by day" (2 Co 4:16).

All this diminishment and growth reaches its natural and spiritual apex in our personal death. Our death is the coincidence of the two interacting movements of God's transforming and consuming love. Death is not extinguishing the light. It is putting out the lamp because the Son is here.

We say "personal death" because the whole person dies, just as the whole person is resurrected. The classical attitude — the body dies, but soul lives on — is incomplete and possibly misleading.[1] The whole person dies: body, soul, emotions, will, mind. And the whole person is transformed out of, through and in death, not just after it.

Of all Jesus's actions during his life — his baptism, his

---

[1]See Ladislaus Boros, *The Mystery of Death*, Herder, 1965; Karl Rahner, *On the Theology of Death* (in *Quaestiones Disputatae Series*), Herder, 1961, also *Theological Investigations*, vols. 7, 11, 13, 18, Seabury, 1977-1983; Roger Troisfontaines, *I Do Not Die*, Desclée, NY, 1963.

transfiguration, his agony in the garden — *the* act of universal salvation was his personal death on the cross. The whole person of the Word incarnate died on Calvary that day. The infinitely perfect theandric act of obedience to his Father and of love for each of us which occurred in Christ's death redeemed us all. Only in death did Jesus's humanity become completely transformed by his divinity.

Our personal death too is our salvific moment par excellence. In our personal death, the paschal mystery of Christ (i.e. his passion, death and resurrection.) reaches the fullness of its redeeming power in us. At that moment when we are weakest — literally reduced to nothing — his transforming activity is strongest and most salvific (2 Co 12:10).

Paradoxically, only in death does each of us become fully human. Until death, we are *becoming* human. In death, we attain the completion of our individual humanity and personality. That principle applies also to the humanity of Jesus. His death and ours is the "moment" in our lives above all others of maximum consciousness, optimum freedom, definitive decision and perfect encounter with God. Thus, death is infinitely more than a separation of body and soul. It marks rather the termination of this mortal life and the passage of the entire person into eternal life, in an act in which we reach the zenith of our individuality and personhood. Death is an integral part of our life. It is essential to life at its fullest. Death is the point of transition between the two basic modes of our one life in Christ Jesus: mortal and immortal, *psychikos* and *pneumatikos* (1 Co 15:44).[2]

We distinguish death from dying. Dying is a lifelong process. Death takes place in an "instant." We begin dying at our inception. Dying ends with death.

Are we active or passive in death? Is death something that we do or is it done to us? The response is: both. Obviously, death is primarily something that happens to us. We undergo it. Yet, there really is something that we must do in our death. We do die. We let our whole self die. We let it happen lovingly, knowingly, willingly.

[2]See *Spiritual Direction*, pp. 25-27, 40-44.

What happens in death? We are referring to *real* death, to the metaphysical reality of death. We are not speaking of just being near death or of witnessing a death. A bystander may observe the before and the after of death — the end of the dying process. Yet, that bystander has not directly witnessed the meta-physical reality of death itself. Neither are we speaking of revival after clinical death. We are not speaking either of the first "death" of Lazarus (Jn 11:11-15) or of the son of the widow of Nain (Lk 7:11-15). Their real death came sometime later.

What happens in the meta-physical, extra-temporal reality of death? Death is the nontemporal transition from time to eternity in which the human person attains maximum consciousness and optimum freedom. Death is the transformation of our present mode of existence. Life is changed, not ended. Death is an integral part of all created existence. Everything has to die in order to become recapitulated in its own way in Christ-Omega.

Death, as nontemporal transition, does not take place in time, even though we use words like "moment" and "instant" of death. Real death is extra-temporal and metaphysical. There is no time-lapse in death. Neither can death be observed, felt or computed in any way.

Death is a kind of compenetration of time and eternity. The last moment of time becomes, so to speak, the first instant of eternity. There is a before death and an after death, but death itself is the transition from one to the other. Time is the measure of motion according to what comes before and what comes after. In time, strictly speaking, there is only past and future. The instant we say "now," it is already past. Eternity, on the other hand, is pure now, *nunc stans*, all-pervading present. Death occurs when my past has completely exhausted my future and all is now — my whole life and person are entirely present. Death is the transition of my whole being from time to eternity.

In death, there is no time, no motion and no quantity. Quantity is the measure of matter in time. In a sense, quantity is space. All processes in this life which involve time, motion, quantity or space are transformed into pure quality in death. This is basically what "spiritualization" means (1 Co 15:44). The processes of knowing, loving and deciding are transposed and compenetrated in death to a state of pure intensity and total presence.

Therefore, in death all mortal limitations are removed and we encounter our Beloved in unrestrained freedom and love. We know him face to face. The full light of day is forevermore. In death, time and motion become dynamic eternity; quantity and space become pure quality; and we become fully ourselves in Father, Son and Spirit. Death is our final threshold of transformation in God. By death we become God by participation in the fullest sense possible. We thus also become spiritually present to the whole of creation, and as perfected instruments of the Father's compassionate love we exert a transforming influence upon the entire Body of Christ.

> *Sic finis viae,*
> *non autem viatoris.*

Appendix 1

St. Teresa of Jesus and Spiritual Genesis

The question arises: How does Teresa of Avila's description of the stages of prayer approximate the thresholds and stages of spiritual genesis which we have presented?

Drawing upon her work *The Interior Castle*, her description of the second mansions or "indwellings" (in which we begin to practice meditation and desire to become more fervent) and the third mansions (in which we continue to advance in discursive prayer and to progress in the Christian life) parallel the threshold and stage of immersion.

The fourth mansions, which describe the beginning of what Teresa terms "passive recollection" and the "prayer of quiet," correlate with the threshold and stage of emergence. These mansions include what St. John of the Cross terms the beginning of contemplation and the night of sense.

What we designate as "personal conversion" corresponds roughly to the fifth mansions wherein the soul enters the "prayer of union."

The sixth mansions of Teresa describe basically the threshold and stage of spiritual espousal.

Finally, the seventh mansions of *The Interior Castle* correspond to spiritual marriage.

Appendix 2

Spiritual Genesis in Relation to Contemporary Developmental Psychology

Over the past few decades, much research has been done in the field of developmental psychology. Some of the more notable authors are Daniel Levinson, Lawrence Kohlberg, Robert Selman, Erik Erikson, Jean Piaget and James Fowler.

Carl Jung, the father of developmental psychology, observes three basic stages in a person's life. The first two of these — which comprise infancy to mid life — he compares to an ascent. Jung likens these two stages to the sun rising in the morning, then steadily climbing until it attains its zenith at high noon. From that point on, it descends. From mid life onward, we too commence to go down. "The descent means the reversal of all the ideals and values that were cherished in the morning."[1]

Describing further our descent, Jung comments: "From the middle of life onward, only he remains vitally alive who is ready *to die with life*. For in the second hour of life's midday the parabola is reversed, death is born. The second half of life does not signify ascent, unfolding, increase, exuberance, but death, since the end is its goal." Jung goes on to insist that to try to avoid this dying is to avoid truly living: "The negation of life's fulfillment is synonymous with refusal to accept its ending. Both mean not wanting to live, and not wanting to live is identical with not wanting to die."[2]

Jung's observations parallel much of what we have included in the thresholds and stages of immersion and emergence. The six authors mentioned above offer other

[1] "The Stages of Life," in *The Structure and Dynamics of the Psyche*, Princeton University Press, 1960, p. 397.

[2] "The Soul and Death," in *op. cit.*, p. 407.

insightful parallels to various aspects of spiritual genesis. We present these basic insights in the following table of optimal parallels.[3] If the reader is familiar with these authors, s/he will understand better the technical terminology. Nonetheless, these parallels should strike a chord in any observant person.

In interpreting the table of optimal parallels, we invite the reader to keep in mind these four preliminary remarks:

1. Each researcher approaches the human person from a different perspective. Kohlberg, for instance, is concerned with the development of moral judgment. Piaget considers the evolution of our cognitive processes. Erikson studies psychosocial maturation, while Fowler researches growth in faith from a phenomenological point of view. In treating spiritual genesis, we have approached the human person holistically, but with specific emphasis on divinization.

2. While we can draw parallels between all these different perspectives, one viewpoint cannot be equated with another. Although there exists profound complementarity between these diverse perspectives, there are no exact equivalents. Moreover, use of a schematic outline necessarily tends to oversimplify each point of view.

3. These parallels are "optimal," or ideal. In reality, few people attain all of them across the board at the same time. Most persons are further advanced in one area than in others at any given stage of their lives.

4. Much work in developmental psychology is closely related to chronological age, although no reputable psychologist adheres rigidily to the age factor. In the spiritual life, however, there is even more flexibility and unpredictability. For some persons certain thresholds of interior development do indeed correspond with their optimal parallels in the chronological eras. For example, the beginning of contemplation may coincide for a given individual with his/her mid-life crisis. However, contemplative prayer could also begin in adolescence for another person. Because of God's freedom to effect his grace within us when and as he wills,

[3]See James Fowler, *Stages of Faith,* Harper and Row, 1981, pp. 52-86, 106-115.

the thresholds and stages of spiritual genesis remain only very loosely associated with the chronological age factor. Yet, a certain basic psychic, emotional and personal maturity is normally presupposed for interior advancement.

One final thought before presenting the table of optimal parallels: It would be rewarding to study from an empirical and structural point of view how advanced spiritual maturity in young persons affects the thresholds they encounter in their psychological maturation. And conversely, it would be revealing to study the effect that interior stagnation has upon the way adults do or do not work through their crises in psychosocial development.

Levinson	Kohlberg	Selman	Spiritual Journey/Genesis			Erikson	Piaget	Fowler
Eras/Approx. Ages	Moral Judgment	Social Role-Taking	Thresholds/Stages	Prayer	Night	Psychosocial Stages	Cognition	Faith
Infancy 0-2			Individual creation		Dark night of the soul	Trust vs. mistrust	Sensorimotor	Undifferentiated faith
Early Childhood 2-6	Punishment/reward Pre-moral	Rudimentary egoistic empathy		Recitation of others' prayers		Autonomy vs. shame/doubt; Initiative vs. guilt	Preoperational	Stage 1: Intuitive-projective faith
Childhood 7-12	Reciprocal fairness	Simple perspective taking		Formal prayers Spontaneous praying		Industry vs. inferiority	Concrete operations	Stage 2: Mythic-literal faith
Adolescence 13-20	Interpersonal expectations and conformity	Mutually interpersonal with certain individuals	Immersion in creation for Christ	Meditation		Identity vs. role confusion	Early formal operations	Stage 3: Synthetic-conventional faith
First Adult Era 20-35	Reflective relativism or class-biased universalism	Mutual with self-chosen groups		Simplified discursive prayer		Intimacy vs. isolation	Formal operations: dichotomizing	Stage 4: Individuative-reflective faith
Middle Adult Era 35-60	Follow a law higher/beyond society's	Mutual with groups, classes, traditions other than one's own	Emergence through creation with Christ Personal conversion	Beginning of contemplation Deepening contemplation	Night of sense Night of spirit	Generativity vs. stagnation	Formal operations: dialectical	Stage 5: Conjunctive faith
Last Adult Era 60 on	Loyalty to a universal ethical principle	Mutually interpersonal with all	Spiritual espousal to Christ; Spiritual Marriage; Personal Death/Resurrection	Advanced contemplation	Tranquil night; Serene night	Integrity vs. despair	Formal operations: synthesizing	Stage 6: Universalizing faith